AF725685

Law and Society
Recent Scholarship

Edited by Melvin I. Urofsky

A Series from LFB Scholarly

Judicial Review of Administrative Discretion

How Justice Scalia and Breyer Regulate the Regulators

Scott Allen Clayton

LFB Scholarly Publishing LLC
El Paso 2015

Copyright © 2015 by LFB Scholarly Publishing LLC

All rights reserved.

Library of Congress Cataloging-in-Publication Data

Clayton, Scott Allen, author.
Judicial review of administrative discretion : how Justices Scalia and Breyer regulate the regulators / Scott Allen Clayton.
pages cm
Includes bibliographical references and index.
ISBN 978-1-59332-801-6 (hardcover : alk. paper)
1. Judicial review of administrative acts--United States. 2. Trade regulation--United States. 3. Scalia, Antonin--Influence. 4. Breyer, Stephen G., 1938---Influence. I. Title.
KF5425.C53 2015
342.73'06--dc23
2015034862

ISBN 978-1-59332-801-6

Manufactured in the United States of America.

Table of Contents

CHAPTER 1

Regulating the Regulators

> If we delegate too much decision making authority to experts, administration and democracy conflict. We lose control. Yet if we delegate too little authority, we also find democracy weakened.
> —Justice Breyer, Active Liberty: Determining our Democratic Constitution

INTRODUCTION

Many public administration scholars have explored the implications of administrative discretion within a democratic and constitutional republic (Davis 1960, 1969; Dodd and Schott 1979; Frederickson 1993; Keiser 1999; Lowi 1979; Schoenbrod 1993; Selden 1997; Selden et al., 1998; Wood and Waterman 1991). Broadly speaking, the focus of these studies is how to control and/or reconcile the concept of power infused within an unelected bureaucracy. An enduring question regarding administrative discretion is how to make the bureaucracy efficient and effective while also ensuring accountability through democratic values of representation and fairness. In other words, how much administrative discretion is appropriate and how best to regulate the regulators?

Friedrich (1940) and Finer (1941) succinctly framed the argument regarding how public administrators should operate and be held accountable within a democracy over 70 years ago. According to Friedrich, the politics-administration dichotomy put forth by Goodnow (1900) was outdated and unrealistic as public administrators routinely and necessarily influence and affect policy. For Friedrich, the demands of government require bureaucratic and technical expertise and call for significant amounts of administrative discretion to ensure government agencies operate effectively. Friedrich advanced a novel approach for his time when he argued the bureaucracy should be primarily accountable to the scientific community and popular sentiment, as opposed to elected officials or what he describes as an ill-defined conception of the will of the state. It follows that under Friedrich's normative accounting of public administration that the boundaries for administrative discretion are necessarily broad and empowering. In fact, Friedrich supports an almost limitless view of administrative discretion when he writes, "within the limits of existing laws, it is the function of the administrator to do everything possible which will make the legislation work" (17).

In response to Friedrich's view, Finer (1941) criticized the concept of an empowered administrator as a way of jeopardizing democratic values and argued that political institutions were obligated and capable of controlling the bureaucracy effectively. As Finer states, "what is needed, however, is not technical capacity per se, but technical capacity in the service of the public welfare as defined by the public and its authorized representatives" (338). In other words, despite agreeing that good governance requires expertise, Finer prefers the "expert on tap and not on top" (348). Moreover, for Finer, there should be a clear line delineating accountability and responsibility that ends with the legislature. Finer recognizes that administrative discretion is inevitable to some extent given vague or impractical laws, but disagrees on how to best address this situation. Instead of empowering the public administrator to help inform and guide policy, Finer calls for, "the continuing control of the representative and judicial agencies" over the bureaucracy (339).

The debate over the limits of administrative discretion continues as many public administration scholars (e.g., Long 1952; Dahl 1970; Appleby 1952; and Frederickson 1997) have advocated Friedrich's view of conferring broad discretionary powers to public administrators while other scholars (e.g., Hyneman 1950; Redford 1969; and Wood and Waterman 1991) emphasize Finer's view of checking administrative discretion through political institutions. Although the question of how much administrative discretion is appropriate is more a question of emphasis and degree than prescription, it is clear that the majority of public administration scholarship has taken the Friedrich approach by supporting the position that broad amounts of administrative discretion is better equipped to achieve good governance. For example, scholars have pointed out on practical grounds that agency's authorizing legislation is often vague and it is impossible to legislate for all possible administrative scenarios, thus requiring a significant amount of administrative discretion to make legislation functional (Bryner 1987; Lipsky 1980; Mazmanian and Sabatier 1989; Prottas 1979; Scott 1997). Similarly, Pierce, Shapiro, and Verkuil (2004) note that when judges override agency decisions, the agency has to begin the policy implementation cycle all over again, which can cause significant delays to needed solutions and there is no guarantee the new decision will produce better results. According to Horowitz (1994), it is more often the case that agencies have a better grasp over the policy in question and the likely effects any decisions would have on policy implementation than does the legislature or courts. Some scholars have shown that oftentimes administrators use their discretionary powers in such a way that the majority of the benefits go directly to the citizenry anyway, thus diminishing the usual counterclaim that granting too much agency discretion leads to abuse of powers (Mosher 1982, Rourke 1984).

In contrast, other scholars such as Lowi (1979) and Schoenbrod (1993) echo Finer's positions by warning that non-elected public administrators are a danger to democracy and have been granted too much discretionary power. According to Lowi (1979), broad discretionary power at the hands of public administrators, "deranges virtually all constitutional relationships and prevents attainment of the constitutional goals of limitation on power, substantive calculability, and procedural calculability" (150). Others, such as Michael Spicer (1995) have argued that reconciling administrative discretion with the Constitution's democratic principles is virtually impossible for public administration scholars to accomplish because of the anti-rationalist worldview shared by the founders that essentially distrusted government and human behavior. Interestingly, Spicer's attempt to deal with the issue of constitutional and administrative legitimacy was addressed through a functional approach towards the Constitution that pushed for bureaucrats to employ common law methods of decision making, similar to how the judicial branch operates.

The path government has taken with respect to these competing views of administrative discretion and accountability in practice is varied as well. On one hand, there is an argument that the Friedrich view carries the day as the growth of government since the New Deal and the corresponding administrative powers following such growth is undeniable. The size and scope of government has continually risen over the years placing numerous responsibilities at the hands of administrators thus resulting in the Friedrich position by-way of default, regardless of any normative theory supporting or refuting this method of governance. In other words, as administrative agencies have grown in size and scope, so too has the use of administrative discretion necessarily grown.

On the other hand, Congress passed the Administrative Procedure Act (APA) in 1946 in response to the growth of government to place limits on agency discretion by creating rules that govern how agencies propose and establish regulations. Among other things, the APA also provides instruction as to when and how federal courts are to review agency decisions and guarantees that "any person suffering legal wrong because of agency action, or adversely affected or aggrieved by agency action within the meaning of a relevant statute, is entitled to judicial review thereof" (5 U.S.C. §§ 702). Moreover, the code of federal regulations has grown to the point that it is published in 221 volumes and exceeds 170,000 pages (many of which govern federal employees directly), giving weight to the argument that both the legislative and executive branch have taken significant steps to mitigate the possibility of abusive agency decision-making through increased regulatory review, processes, and law. These measures more closely align to Finer's view of endorsing external political checks on the bureaucracy.

Contemporary scholarship on the topic of administrative discretion has moved from the argument over legislative and administrative supremacy and is primarily focused on how to keep bureaucrats accountable using internal and external methods. For example, scholars have called for increased institutional checks such as legislative and judicial oversight, as well as improved administrative ethics and organizational structure. Another approach, termed representative bureaucracy, attempts to explain the use of administrative discretion though preferences stemming from race, ethnicity, and gender. For example, according to Selden and Sowa (2007), the theory of representative bureaucracy maintains that, "a more representative workforce can lead to discretion being exercised toward the achievement of policy outcomes that are more representative and responsive to particular groups, especially minority groups" (703). Rohr (1986) takes a slightly different approach towards representative bureaucracy using the Constitution when he points out that there are disproportionately small numbers of members within the House of Representatives (435 members) as compared to the general U.S. population (over 300 million people)—which has grown tremendously since the country's inception—thus requiring bureaucrats to further represent and give voice to the people to meet the constitutional expectations of representation espoused by the founders.

In addition to the executive and legislative branch, the judicial branch also influences the role of the bureaucracy. Central to this research endeavor is how the Supreme Court has attempted to try and strike the appropriate balance of agency discretion and political accountability. First a quick discussion on the term "discretion" is in order to clarify how this book will evaluate judicial review of administrative actions.

Many scholars have recognized that the term discretion has different meanings in different contexts (Friendly, 1982; Shapiro, 1983; Koch, 1986). According to Koch (1986), there are as many as 5 types of discretionary actions taken on behalf of administrative agencies. These include, "individualized discretion", "executing discretion", "policymaking discretion", "unbridled discretion", and "numinous discretion". Koch explains the first three types are what courts typically review as they involve decisions such as adjusting the agency rules to fit a particular circumstance (individualized), filling-in gaps of ambiguous authorizing statutes (executing), and creating rules to further the aim or mission of the agency and authorizing statute (policymaking). Unbridled discretion refers to instances of discretion that the Courts are not allowed to review according to statute, and numinous discretion refers to acts of discretion which by its very nature is inaccessible to the courts. However, even in the latter two cases, it is possible for the courts to review other factors that may affect the core discretionary decision.

Warren (2011) describes administrative discretion as part of a theoretical continuum where on one side of the spectrum are formal agency actions that are purely non-discretionary and are those actions solely based on following formal procedure codes, statutes, rules, or court orders. On the other side of the spectrum are informal agency actions that are solely based on an administrator's discretion. Warren points out that in practice agency actions are never completely controlled by formal procedural codes or dominated by an administrator's discretion, but fall somewhere on the continuum. In other words, the more agency actions are controlled by administrative discretion, the more the agency action is considered informal and vice versa (314). Warren gives some examples of informal-discretionary actions including; initiating, prosecuting, negotiating, settling, contracting, dealing, advising, threatening, publicizing, concealing, planning, recommending, supervising, as well as the decision to not perform any of these or similar such actions. (315).

For Davis (1969) administrative discretion takes root when, the effective limits on [an official's] power leave him free to make a choice among possible courses of action or inaction. This definition of administrative discretion is fairly broad, but it takes into account the subtle distinction between informal and formal actions noted above while also leaving room to assess how an agency goes about interpreting their authorizing statute(s). An administrator's attempt to interpret and apply statutory language is a critical administrative function, but the act of interpretation does not neatly conform to either categorization of informal or formal action because the law as written is the very source of an agency's formal authority and responsibility—giving rise to formal and nondiscretionary actions, yet the act of interpretation is oftentimes by nature a subjective endeavor—giving rise to informal and discretionary action. Therefore, to capture a broad understanding of how discretion applies to both action and interpretation, this book uses Davis's definition of discretion as a starting point to assess how Breyer and Scalia go about depicting where the boundaries of such "effective limits" are placed with respect to administrative discretion.

Supreme Court and Judicial Review

Broadly speaking, the extent to which the Supreme Court influences public administration has been documented different ways by various scholars in the field of public administration (Cann 1995; Cooper 2007; Horowitz 1977; Lee and Rosenbloom 2005; Newbold 2010; Rosenbloom 2003; Rohr 1998). Some scholars, such as Cooper and

Horowitz have gone as far to say that the courts have at times "judicialized" the administrative process by requiring agencies to essentially mirror the courts hearing procedures. Similarly, Cann writes that the courts are by default responsible for controlling the bureaucracy because the president lacks the raw power to do so, and Congress generally lacks the will to do so (1995, xxiii). Unlike the congressional and executive branches, the courts serve as the final arbiter in interpreting and applying legislation and agency regulations to decipher whether an agency action is in fact lawful. In other words, the courts are in the position of setting precedent for how much and under what circumstances administrative discretion is appropriate. However, the institutional voice of the Court has been inconsistent and has changed over time regarding the topic of judicial review and administrative discretion.

Going back over 200 years, the Supreme Court famously held in the landmark *Marbury v. Madison*, 5 U.S. 137 (1803) that "it is emphatically the province and duty of the judicial department to say what the law is" (5 U.S.137). However, after the New Deal and prior to the passage of the APA, the Supreme Court has decided cases in ways that confuse this seemingly straightforward pronouncement. For example, cases such as *Gray v. Powell*, 314 U.S. 402 (1941) and *NLRB v. Hearst Publications, Inc.*, 322 U.S. 111 (1944) both held that the courts should defer to agency interpretations of statutes for those statutes the agency is charged with implementing, thus distinguishing the larger notion of judicial review for all statutes. However, this narrowed view has also been at odds with other Court opinions. For example, in *United States v. American Trucking Assns., Inc.,* 310 U.S. 534 (1940) the majority opinion states, "The interpretation of the meaning of statutes, as applied to justiciable controversies, is exclusively a judicial function" (1064). Similarly, the subsequent *Skidmore v. Swift & Co.*, 323 U.S. 134 (1944) decision points out that agency rulings, interpretations, and opinions of the administrator do not control judicial decision and do not constitute an interpretation of the Act or a standard for judging factual situations. Writing in 1955, Bernard Schwartz summed up the confusion when he writes the Supreme Court has been "inconsistent in its application" regarding precedent binding administrative discretion such that it "has led to the belief that the Court in this field has been guided by purely discretionary factors by the arbitrary whims and caprices of the majority of the justices" (1955, 1-2).

Since the passage of the APA, the institutional voice of the Court has not proved much more consistent regarding judicial review and administrative discretion. According to Eskridge and Baer, the "Supreme Court's deference jurisprudence is a mess," and moreover "to the extent the Court does follow an 'approach', it is ad hoc" (2008, 1057). To some extent the APA calls for the courts to give effect to a broad interpretation of judicial review, requiring in section 706 that, "to the extent necessary to decision and when presented, the reviewing court shall decide all relevant questions of law, interpret constitutional and statutory provisions, and determine the meaning or applicability of the terms of an agency action." In addition, section 706 of the APA makes clear the courts may review any administrative action to determine whether it was "arbitrary, capricious, [or] an abuse of discretion." Perhaps not surprisingly though, the Court's attempt to apply those value laden terms in practice has varied over the years and the Court has established, held, distinguished, and even reversed its own precedents along the way. Just a few cases to show how the Court has evolved regarding the topic of judicial review of administrative discretion since the passage of the APA are noted below.

- *Citizens to Preserve Overton Park v. Volpe*, 401 U.S. 402 (1971) This case gave life to the APA's arbitrary and capricious standard by both defining substantive limits of administrative power with respect to the authorizing statute, and calling for agencies to undergo all possible alternatives in the decision-making/rule-making process with respect to the intention of the statute prior to issuing a rule.
- *Motor Vehicle Mfrs. Association v. State Farm Ins.*, 463 U.S. 29 (1983) The arbitrary and capricious standard was reshaped to primarily focus on the adequacy of the agency procedures and decision making process and less so the substance of the agency discretion/rule employed.
- *Chevron U.S.A., Inc. v. Natural Resources Defense Council, Inc.*, 467 U.S. 837 (1984). This case put forth a two-step rule for determining judicial review of administrative agencies. Namely, if the courts determine the authorizing statute is

ambiguous, then the courts should defer to the agency's interpretation of the statute, so long as the agency's interpretation is permissible.

- *United States v. Mead Corporation*, 533 U.S. 218 (2001). The Court distinguished *Chevron* such that if an agency is not exercising delegated lawmaking power, then the courts must interpret the meaning of the authorizing statute and not the agency (discussed more below).

Since *United States v. Mead Corporation* 533 U.S. 218 (2001) (hereafter *Mead*) was handed down, a host of legal articles have pointed out the inconsistent approach the Court has since applied regarding judicial review of administrative discretion (Bressman 2005; Levin 2002; Vermeule 2003). To say the least, the quest to define the proper limits of administrative discretion is an enduring, albeit elusive endeavor. Not only have theoreticians wrestled with the normative implications of administrative discretion, but the legislative, executive, and judicial branch have also struggled to formulate a model for administrative discretion that meets both practical and democratic expectations.

Knowing the institutional voice of the Court has changed over the years—and will likely continue to do so—this book takes a more nuanced approach than simply reviewing the Court at large and instead compares how two Supreme Court Justices (Scalia and Breyer) have attempted to place the proper role and limitations regarding administrative discretion through their Court opinions covering administrative law. The decision to focus on Justice Breyer and Scalia as the focal points for this book stems from their renowned interest and expertise on the subject of administrative law as well as their well documented and contrasting views on legal reasoning and statutory interpretation discussed more in depth in chapter 2.

To set the stage for the remainder of this book, a quick look at a few cases demonstrating the varied approaches both Scalia and Breyer have applied regarding the topic of judicial review and administrative discretion are detailed next. These examples highlight unique approaches in how they both review agency actions.

First, in June 2001, the Supreme Court decided *Mead* to determine whether a tariff classification ruling by the United States Customs

Service deserves judicial deference. Under the Harmonized Tariff Schedule of the United States (HTSUS), the United States Customs Service is authorized to classify and fix the rate of duty on imports under rules and regulations issued by the Secretary of the Treasury. Under the Secretary's regulations, any port-of-entry Customs office and the Customs Headquarters Office may issue "ruling letters" setting tariff classifications for particular imports. The Respondent in this case, the Mead Corporation, imported "day planners," three-ring binders with pages having room for notes of daily schedules, phone numbers, addresses, and a calendar.

Between 1989 and 1993, Customs categorized day planners as "other" and thus did not subject these items to a tariff of 4.0%, as applied to a similar category that included diaries, bounded notebooks and address books, memorandum pads, letter pads and similar articles. In January 1993, however, Customs changed its position, and issued a Headquarters ruling letter classifying Mead's day planners as "Diaries ..., bound" subject to the 4.0% tariff. Subsequently, Mead filed suit in the Court of International Trade whereby the court granted to government summary judgment. The Court of Appeals reversed, finding that ruling letters should not be treated like Customs regulations—which receive the highest level of deference—because they are not preceded by notice-and-comment as under the Administrative Procedure Act (APA), do not carry the force of law, and are not intended to clarify importers' rights and obligations beyond the specific case.

The Supreme Court held in an 8-1 opinion authored by Justice Souter, that the case at hand did not warrant judicial deference of administrative discretion. The Court clarified that the administrative implementation of a particular statutory provision qualifies for *Chevron*[1] deference when it appears that Congress delegated authority to the agency generally to make rules carrying the force of law, and that the interpretation claiming deference was promulgated in the exercise of that authority. The Court vacated the judgment and remanded the case for further proceedings in light of the new standard set forth by the Court.

The Court's decision was significant in that it distinguished the precedent set by *Chevron* almost 20 years prior regarding the extent to which the Court should defer to agency decision making—a central issue within the field of public administration. However, the lone dissent authored by Justice Scalia was relevant for both public administration theoreticians and practitioners as it goes beyond merely arguing against the decision and reasoning of the majority opinion, but also expresses a concern for the future of public administrators and the lower courts who try to implement the newfound Court doctrine regarding administrative discretion. Justice Scalia plainly states in his dissent that the majority opinion is, "neither sound in principle nor sustainable in practice," and then goes on to convey sensitivity to the difficulties and complexities facing public administrators in the 21st century when he writes,

> "But in an era when federal statutory law administered by federal agencies is pervasive, and when the ambiguities (intended or unintended) that those statutes contain are innumerable, totality-of-the-circumstances *Skidmore*[2] deference is a recipe for uncertainty, unpredictability, and endless litigation. To condemn a vast body of agency action to that regime (all except rulemaking, formal (and informal?) adjudication, and whatever else might now and then be included within today's intentionally vague formulation of affirmative congressional intent to "delegate") is irresponsible." (250)

Justice Scalia's substantive arguments regarding public administration as put forth in his dissent can be briefly summarized as follows:

- Reasonable agency application of an ambiguous statutory provision should be sustained so long as it represented the agency's authoritative interpretation.
- When Congress leaves an ambiguity in a statute that is to be administered by an executive agency, it should be presumed that Congress meant to give the agency discretion, within the limits of reasonable interpretation, as to how the ambiguity is to be resolved.
- The innumerable statutory ambiguities facing administrators in the 21st century demands that agencies have reasonable discretionary powers to effectively operate.

- Judicial resolutions of administrative decisions are final and thus less amenable to change over time. The result of increased judicial oversight—in place of administrative discretion—prevents agencies from flexibly adapting rules as political moods shift and new information develops over time that may better inform practice.

In the second example—moving forward to 2005—the Court decided *National Cable and Telecommunication Association v. Brand X Internet Services* 545 U.S. 967 (2005), (hereafter *National Cable*) a similar case that determined whether or not the Federal Communications Commission's (FCC) statutory interpretation of Title II of the Communications Act of 1934 was permissible. The FCC concluded that cable companies selling broadband Internet service do not provide "telecommunications service" as the Communications Act defines the term and hence are exempt from mandatory common-carrier regulation. The Court held in a 6-3 decision that FCC's interpretation was lawful and thus deferred to the agency. In this case, Scalia did not defer to the agency interpretation of the statute as he did in *Mead,* partially fueling this research project by begging the question, why not?

National Cable is notable for many reasons, namely because the case held that an agency continues to have discretion to exercise lawmaking power delegated by Congress even after a court interprets the meaning of an ambiguous statute, but it is introduced here to point out Breyer's concurring-majority opinion which specifically takes aim at Scalia's dissent as well as Scalia's previous dissent in *Mead.* Justice Breyer offers a differing opinion on the resultant implications stemming from the *Mead* case on public administration and re-emphasizes the intention behind the *Mead* majority opinion (which Breyer joined) that contrasts Scalia's description. Breyer's concurring opinion reiterated the intent of the majority opinion in *Mead* by summarizing three major points.

- An agency action qualifies for *Chevro*n deference when Congress has explicitly or implicitly delegated to the agency the authority to "fill" a statutory "gap," including an interpretive gap created through an ambiguity in the language of a statute's provisions.

- Such delegation "may be shown in a variety of ways, as by an agency's power to engage in adjudication or notice-and-comment rule making, or by some other indication of a comparable congressional intent."
- The existence of a formal rulemaking proceeding is neither a necessary nor a sufficient condition for according *Chevron* deference to an agency's interpretation of a statute.

Breyer's re-emphasis on the majority opinion of *Mead* puts forth a less rule-bound approach than Scalia, whereby the judicial branch has more discretion to determine what circumstances call for judicial review of administrative agency actions. For example, as stated above, determining whether Congress "implicitly" intended for an agency to promulgate rules necessarily requires some level of judgment. Similarly, the second point which states that such delegation may be shown in a variety of ways, including, "…some other indication of a comparable congressional intent," without specifically defining what those indications might include opens the door for various interpretations. Finally, the last point shows that a formal rulemaking proceeding is "neither a necessary or sufficient condition," reiterating that the courts are on their own in determining what conditions call for judicial review of administrative agency actions. In short, all of the factors above support a loose standard for courts to follow when determining whether judicial deference to agency decisions and interpretations of law are justified.

On the surface, both approaches seem to offer strengths and challenges for ensuring public administrators operate within the confines of the Constitution. On one hand is a push for a clear set of rules that will allow administrative agencies the opportunity to leverage their subject matter expertise over time and in new ways to best meet their statutory obligations. On the other hand is a push to ensure that the judicial branch does not arbitrarily limit itself from performing an important check on administrative agencies.

Based on Breyer's explanation of the *Mead* case, it seems his jurisprudence aligns with Finer's preference for judicial checks on administrative agencies, whereas Scalia seems to align with Friedrich given his willingness to assume that Congress intends for agencies to have discretion over any ambiguity in authorizing statues. However,

Breyer's decision to defer to the agency and Scalia's decision to overturn the agency interpretation in the *National Cable* case suggests there are other distinguishing factors between these Justices' jurisprudence which may also affect their willingness to defer to administrative agencies, discussed next.

Interestingly, the case of *National Cable* primarily turned on the Justices' statutory interpretation of how to best define the meaning of the word "offer" as it relates to the Communications Act. Although Breyer and Scalia reach differing opinions, both Justices' reasoning appear consistent with the method of jurisprudence they claim to endorse in their books and extrajudicial writings. For example, Justice Scalia's 1997 book, *A Matter of Interpretation: Federal Courts and the Law,* explains how his method of statutory and constitutional interpretation (i.e., "textualism" and "originalism" respectively, discussed more in chapter 2) derives meaning from the text as understood during the time it was written which then helps prevent excessive use of judge made law to preserve democracy and the political process. Similarly, Breyer has put forth his method of legal reasoning in various articles and most notably in his 2005 book, *Active Liberty: Interpreting our Democratic Constitution* (which some claim was written in direct response to Scalia's 1997 book) and subsequent 2010 book, *Making Our Democracy Work: A Judges View*, wherein he puts forth a legal philosophy that is pragmatic and aimed at capturing the spirit of the law while also helping to encourage citizens to participate in democracy. In short, Breyer advocates for the "Living Constitution" method of jurisprudence which empowers judges to assess the values of the Constitution in relation to the ever changing times. In addition to text, history, tradition, and precedent (tools both Justices claim to use as part of their legal reasoning), Breyer also claims to consider the "purpose" and "consequences" of laws and decisions as part of his legal reasoning as well as the "legislative history" surrounding the passage of laws to help discern what constitutes those purposes. Breyer also cites international courts in support of his opinions whereas Scalia claims to not do so.

Considering the Justices' purported theories of legal reasoning and statutory interpretation along with the *Mead* and *National Cable* decisions described above, makes for an interesting intersection of ideas as shared between Friedrich/Scalia and Finer/Breyer on the topic of administrative discretion. For example, all of the bulleted points above outlining Scalia's reasoning for his dissent in the *Mead* case suggests that he advocates for minimal judicial intervention of agency decisions and thus affords broad discretionary powers for administrative agencies. This view conforms with Friedrich's approach of calling for empowered administrators who are primarily responsible to the scientific community, technical experts, and professional standards as opposed to external political entities. Thus, it is likely that Friedrich would agree with Scalia that an external check such as judicial review of administrative discretion is not the ideal solution in most instances. However, Scalia's willingness to overturn the agency interpretation of a statute in the *National Cable* case can be traced to his method of jurisprudence which calls for a "textualist" interpretation of the statute, along with his method of legal reasoning (formalism, discussed more in chapter 2). Interestingly, Scalia's method of applying a formal set of rules to adjudicate more closely resembles not that of Friedrich, but Finer, as Finer advocates for the politics/administration dichotomy and strict separation of powers and adherence to codified rules and laws as methods to ensure checks on administrative discretion.

Similarly, Breyer's position calling for increased judicial oversight of administrative discretion aligns with Finer's view that legislative and judicial checks are necessary to prevent administrative abuse of discretion. Yet, whereas Scalia and Finer used the same analytical tools (e.g., formalism, rules, and clear boundaries) to support different conclusions regarding the role of administrative discretion; Breyer and Finer use opposite tools to arrive at the same conclusion. For example, Breyer's method of jurisprudence indicates a less rule bound and less formal approach that emphasizes purpose, consequences, and situational or case by case adjudication, whereas Finer supports the opposite approach of a politics/administration dichotomy and the formal separation of powers. Yet, both claim to use these contrasting methods as a way to preserve legislative and judicial checks on administrative agencies.

Based on the aforementioned, a close look at how Friedrich and Finer intersect with Scalia and Breyer presents some interesting questions on the topic of administrative discretion. Namely, is it the case that a less rule bound approach provided by Breyer and Friedrich actually results in more judicial deference to agency decisions when exploring Breyer's opinions, despite Breyer and Scalia arguments to the contrary? On a related note, how is Scalia and Finer's preference for a strong executive branch affected by a textualist method of constitutional and statutory interpretation as applied in Scalia opinions? Exploring these Justices' varied approaches offers some practical guidance as to how administrative discretion is enabled or constrained through their different approaches. Given public administrators are also charged with interpreting and applying authorizing statutes, a review of how Justice Breyer's and Scalia's theory meets practice provides some practical guidance for practitioners to consider as well.

As stated above, a supplemental theme of this project is to augment public administration theories that have tried to make sense of how the Supreme Court affects public administration (Cann 1995; Cooper 2007; Horowitz 1977; Lee and Rosenbloom 2005; Rosenbloom 2003; Rohr 1998). More specifically, the first aim of this research project is to determine whether Justice Scalia and Justice Breyer's rhetoric and stated positions on legal reasoning and statutory interpretation hold true when specifically analyzing administrative law cases on the subject of administrative discretion.

The research findings place both Justices' jurisprudence within public administration literature that focuses on administrative discretion in various ways, such as through administrative leadership, administrative and democratic values, and political accountability and representativeness. Each of these concepts are to some extent embodied by the Friedrich-Finer debates, but a few examples are noted below to show how implications from the above opinions regarding administrative law and legal theory fuse with contemporary scholarship on the subject, including Larry Terry's theory of conservatorship (2003), David Rosenbloom's legislative centered public administration (2000), and John Rohr's theory of representative bureaucracy (1986).

Breyer's and Scalia's jurisprudence and extrajudicial writings also indicate that their legal philosophies both contradict and support varying aspects of the aforementioned public administrative theorists' accounting of administrative discretion through closely related sub-topics such as the proper role of the courts, separation of powers, and statutory interpretation in unique ways. For example, Terry agrees with Breyer that Justice Scalia's method of constitutional interpretation (i.e., originalism) is a poor method for administrators to follow as it is, "based on a flawed assumption that one can interpret the intentions of the founders with a certain degree of mechanical precision"(2003, 68). For Terry, this method of statutory interpretation limits an administrative conservator's ability to preserve mission by constraining the discretion of agency decision-makers. Similar to Friedrich, Terry's theory of conservatorship is premised on the notion that, "the delegation of broad discretionary power to administrative officials is essential if they are to pursue and protect the public interest" (2003, xiv).

In contrast, Justice Scalia's describes his concept of "originalism" as a way to limit judicial oversight of administrative agencies, thus conferring broad administrative discretion to public administrative officials. In other words, Justice Scalia envisions his interpretive method of originalism as the most likely approach to achieve what Terry demands—empowered administrators with broad discretionary powers to protect the public interest. For Justice Scalia, judges are much less equipped to make highly specialized decisions and should therefore defer to agency decisions so long as the decisions are reasonable and within the purview of the authorizing legislation (1978). Although both Justice Scalia and Terry agree that administrative discretion is essential, they are not of the same mind when it comes to how to best preserve and empower such discretionary authority. This book explores Justice Scalia's opinions further and offers up some examples as to whether or not the method of originalism Scalia claims to employ in action actually preserves or limits administrative power and adaptability.

Another conflict of means resulting in similar ends was found in the way Scalia, Breyer, Terry (2003) and Rohr (1986) view the separation of powers doctrine and how this doctrine affects the legitimacy of the administrative state, and hence administrative discretion. For Rohr, the concept of a strict separation of powers is misplaced and has created an unnecessary threat towards legitimizing public administration and administrative discretion byway of the Constitution. Rohr recognizes that the bureaucracy is not directly accountable to democratic elections and the role of the administrative state is not explicitly discussed in the Constitution, creating a democratic and constitutional conundrum of sorts for the legitimacy of administrative rulemaking. Rohr sets out to correct this problem of constitutional legitimacy by demonstrating that the founders never intended a strict separation of powers, but instead envisioned that each branch of governance should incorporate within itself some blending of shared powers, similar to the shared powers found in administrative agencies which often possess rulemaking (legislative), managerial (executive), and adjudicatory (judicial) functions to varying degrees. Rohr argues that the similarity found between the three branches of government and administrative agencies all having shared powers, offers some support in reconciling the unelected bureaucracy with the Constitution. One method Rohr used to support his case was to introduce evidence of legislative history, such as floor debates, failed proposals, and various discussions held about the Constitution during the founding period that suggest the founders never intended to advocate for a formalized and strict separation of powers doctrine. Similarly, Terry (2003) argues that administrative executives should "know the specific and general legislative history of an agency's legal mandates" (84). Terry goes as far as suggesting that state executives who may not have access to the legislative history of their agency—due to states often having limited documentation—actually take steps to understand the authorizing legislation by "contact[ing] the sponsor directly to obtain historical information and ascertain what he or she had in mind" (84-85).

In contrast, Justice Scalia has continuously argued against the use of legislative history as a means to understand the meaning of laws or the Constitution. In Justice Scalia's words,

> "The greatest defect of legislative history is its illegitimacy. We are governed by laws, not by the intentions of legislators. . . . But not the least of the defects of legislative history is its indeterminacy. If one were to search for an interpretative technique that, on the whole, was more likely to confuse than to clarify, one could hardly find a more promising candidate than legislative history." (1988, 38)

Justice Scalia's contrasting perception of the strict separation of powers doctrine insists that clear boundaries are the primary ingredient to preserving a democratic republic. For Scalia, "it is the structure of government, its constitution, in the real sense of that word, that ultimately preserves or destroys freedom" (1988). Smith (1993) describes Justice Scalia's stance on separation of powers as though,

> "any deviation, no matter how minor or apparently inconsequential, from the strict boundaries that separate the authority and functions of the respective branches of government may ultimately lead to the excessive accumulation of power in a single branch and thereby threaten individual liberty". (41)

Thus, for Justice Scalia, it follows that any attempt to legitimate the administrative state with the Constitution must first come to terms with a strict separation of powers, and must do so by looking within the four corners of the document itself, without relying on legislative history.

Breyer takes a more pragmatic approach towards the separation of powers that is amenable to Rohr's view, and has specifically advocated for the use of legislative history such as floor debates and written proposals in an attempt to understand the Congress's intent. According to Breyer, a Judge is right to look at the background of a statute, the terms of the debate over its enactment, the factual assumptions the legislators made, the conventions they thought applicable, and their expressed objectives in an effort to understand the statute's relevant context, conventions, and purposes (1992, 848). The review of Breyer's opinions will give some insight as to how the legislative background and process may impact his decisions and whether the legislative history tends to support his decision to empower or limit administrative actions and/or interpretations under review by the Court.

Finally, Rosenbloom's (2000) legislative centered public administration theory intersects with Scalia's and Breyer's approach in unique ways. Rosenbloom shows how administrative agencies are grounded and held accountable by the legislature, and that since the passage of the APA in 1946, administrative agencies function as "extensions of Congress with the legislature as supervisors of the agency" (5). Reminiscent of Finer's position, Rosenbloom says that Congress should and does provide an institutional check on administrative discretion, and that administrative agencies should emphasize legislative values such as representation, participation, and open information above managerial values such as efficiency, economy, organizational effectiveness, and "unity of command" practices formerly endorsed during the progressive era (2000, 5).

Given Scalia's stated position that the judiciary should defer to agency decisions in most cases[3], it follows that Justice Scalia perceives the legislature and administrative agencies as very closely fused together, but out of necessity instead of principle. In other words, if the legislature wants to effectively manage the bureaucracy then Congress needs to write laws in such a way that legislative intent and policy implementation can effectively unite. Justice Scalia agrees with Rosenbloom regarding the necessarily close connection between Congress and the administrative state, however, he does so for different reasons.

Breyer's espoused legal theory suggests that he would agree with Rosenbloom's assessment of ensuring legislative values are prioritized over managerial values. Moreover, Breyer's call for judicial checks on administrative decisions would suggest agreement with the idea of legislative oversight of administrative agencies. However, it is not clear that Justice Breyer would go as far as Scalia or Rosenbloom in calling for Congress to write more detailed laws. In fact Justice Breyer has pointed to the opposite problem when he writes,

> "Statutes that tell administrators precisely which pollutants to regulate, and where and how to regulate them, can prove similarly counterproductive. The legislator who tries to become a super-detailed air pollution regulator can easily end up with dirtier air." (2010, 116)

Similar to Rosenbloom's description of legislative checks on the bureaucracy, Breyer argues for increased judicial review of agency decisions thus also placing greater emphasis on the value of institutional checks on administrative power and decisions. For Breyer, the Court is right to review agency decisions depending on the "...statute's purposes and context, and particularly on matters of comparative expertise" (2010, 118). In other words, the courts need to determine who is better situated to answer the statutory ambiguity, the agency or the court? To resolve this question, Breyer argues that the

Judge should ask themselves, how would a reasonable legislator answer the question? (2005, 106)

Regime Values

The value of a comparative analysis between two highly regarded Supreme Court Justices on the subject of administrative law is tied to Rohr's broader assessment of the value of studying Supreme Court cases generally. According to Rohr, the best route for understanding the proper role for public administration is to understand the US government's "regime values" so that public administrators can then uphold those values. For Rohr, the best way for public administrators to identify and understand the meaning of America's central values is to study Supreme Court constitutional decisions given they are institutional, pertinent, concrete, and dialectic. The research employed for this book evaluates each Justice's opinions through the lens of Rohr's pillars (i.e., dialectic, institutional, pertinent, and concrete) discussed more in chapter 2 explaining why the Court is an ideal source to understand regime values. By using Rohr's pillars, the research will elucidate how judicial themes identified can inform administrative discretion and thus public administration theory and practice. For example, how does Scalia's and Breyer's administrative law jurisprudence depict a constitutionally competent public administrator and what are the similarities, differences, and challenges posed by both of these Justices for public administrators? Or, as Lee and Rosenbloom (2005) have phrased, how do these opinions help practitioners determine, what is a *reasonable public servant*?

Design

The research design used for this book is a descriptive and historical case study analysis of primary documents gathered from Justice Scalia and Breyer on the subject of administrative law, and specifically the topic of administrative discretion. To a much lesser extent, cases in which these Justices voted but did not contribute to the written opinion are also mentioned. In addition to Supreme Court opinions, the research supplements themes found from the case briefings with their extrajudicial writings such as academic law review articles, books, and documented speaking engagements.

A historical case-briefing analysis was chosen for this research endeavor because of the availability of primary source documents. Legal opinions, books, academic articles, and opinion papers have been authored by both Justices identifying themes of jurisprudence that can be measured against their administrative law jurisprudence specifically.

Case Selection

The primary methodological question facing this project is how to best select the administrative law cases related to administrative discretion for review. Westlaw was the research database used herein to identify and select cases for this project. Westlaw offers the researcher a myriad of ways to select cases, including a "key-search" option that categorizes types of cases heard by the Supreme Court with a category for administrative law and numerous subcategories such as jurisdiction, regulations and rule-making, de novo review, judicial review, and adjudication, to name just a few. A few subcategories such as "discretion of administrative agency" and "arbitrary and capricious standard of review", seemed especially relevant to the purposes of this review. However, there were only 3 cases heard by the Supreme Court during Breyer's and Scalia's shared time on the bench that were categorized under the arbitrary and capricious standard, and only 5 cases categorized under the discretion of administrative agency label. Also, the research found there is considerable overlap in how Westlaw categorizes cases. For example, 1 of the 5 cases categorized under discretion of administrative agency was also labeled under the arbitrary and capricious standard categorization. Moreover, not all cases that are known to have some impact on administrative discretion were included under the subcategories stated above. For example the *Mead* case introduced earlier which distinguished *Chevron*—thus arguably one of the most impactful cases concerning judicial review of administrative discretion—was not included in the "discretion of administrative agency" categorization.

To account for the various ways Westlaw categorizes and organizes cases, the key-cite method used for this project was broadened to include all "administrative law cases" during Scalia's and

Breyer's time on the Supreme Court whereby one of them authored a majority, dissenting, or concurring opinion. This approach ensures that any substantive cases whereby Scalia or Breyer wrote an opinion on the topic of administrative review are not missed due to Westlaw's extensive sub-categorization method.

Using the broad-net approach of querying all administrative law cases resulted in 27 possible cases to review for Justice Scalia and 22 possible cases to review for Justice Breyer. However, there was some overlap as 7 of the cases were shared between both Scalia and Breyer as they both authored an opinion for the case (*F.C.C. v. Fox Television stations, Inc; Christensen v. Harris County; Shalala v. Illinois Council on Long Term Care, Inc.; Federal Election Commission v. Akins;* and *Coeur Alaska, Inc. v. Southeast Alaska Conservation Council; City of Arlington, Texas v. F.C.C* and *Utility Air Regulatory Group v. E.P.A*). The limited number of administrative law cases allowed the researcher to review each case and determine cases that were most relevant to the practice of public administration. For the purposes of this work, cases whereby the Court was determining whether an agency's specific actions (and inactions) or agency's interpretation of its authorizing statute—thus affecting agency action and discretion—were considered relevant and selected for review.

Administrative law cases that were not selected for review turned on legal questions that have limited discernible impact or value for public administrators, such as whether an individual has legal standing to bring a case forward under law regardless of any particular agency action, the relation of state laws and potentially pre-emptive federal statutes, third party standing to bring suit regardless of any particular agency action, standing under the "supremacy clause", and whether a case is "ripe" for review. Similarly, cases that questioned whether or not the very agency itself is in fact constitutional and 1st amendment cases that did not focus on any particular administrative action (or interpretation of authorizing legislation) were not included. See Appendix for the list of cases that were removed along with a brief synopsis of why they were not especially relevant for this project. It is important to note that for each of these cases no agency actions were at issue, or if so, they were not addressed by the Court but remanded to lower courts for further proceedings.

After removing the cases noted in the Appendix there were a total of 14 possible cases to review for Scalia and 10 possible cases to review for Breyer. However, 5 cases (*Christensen v. Harris County*; *F.C.C. v. Fox Television stations, Inc.; Coeur Alaska, Inc. v. Southeast Alaska Conservation Council, City of Arlington, Texas v. F.C.C;* and *Utility Air Regulatory Group v. E.P.A.* were cases that both Justice Scalia and Breyer authored an opinion. Thus, a total of 19 cases were selected for review.[4]

Roadmap of Book

The remainder of the book is organized as follows. Chapter 2 provides an overview of each Justice to show some of the prevailing views regarding both Justices' opinions and approach to their role as a Judge, especially concerning their political leanings, method of legal reasoning, method of statutory and constitutional interpretation, and even their personality that will help set the stage for understanding how to best assess their administrative law jurisprudence on the topic of administrative discretion. Chapter 2 also includes a discussion on formalism and legal realism as these concepts are central to understanding the methods of legal reasoning each Justice purports to follow. Finally, Chapter 2 concludes with a description of Rohr's "regime values", the academic linchpin used to explain the benefits of placing and understanding the implications of Justice Scalia's and Breyer's jurisprudence on the subject of administrative discretion as it relates to public administration theory and practice.

Chapters 3-6 begins the case-briefing analysis of Scalia and Breyer opinions on the subject of administrative discretion. Instead of simply dedicating a chapter to Scalia opinions and another chapter to Breyer opinions spanning across multiple issue areas, the cases are presented by subject matter to help the reader follow the intricacies of similarly situated cases and better decipher the distinguishing factors that often lead to differing opinions. For the most part, the cases are grouped together by the federal agency under review by the Court. For example, chapter 3 begins with five cases involving the Food and Drug Administration, Federal Communications Commission, and the Securities and Exchange Commission. Chapter 4 reviews six cases concerning the Environmental Protection Agency, including some of its subsidiary agencies. Chapter 5 takes a look at four cases stemming from the Department of Labor, and Chapter 6 finishes the case-briefings by analyzing two cases focusing on the Department of Justice and one case regarding the Internal Revenue Service. In addition to the standard case briefing methodology employed, chapters 3-6 will also interject supplemental and extra-juridical writings as well as prior and related cases.

Chapter 7 begins the analysis of Justice Scalia's and Breyer's jurisprudence as related to public administration scholarship on the topic of administrative discretion and democratic values. This section carves out values and guidance that these Justices' administrative law jurisprudence has to offer the field of public administration. The themes are then connected and contrasted with one another to understand the strengths and challenge their jurisprudence places on public administrators. To do this, the analysis first tracks and charts salient factors related to their method of legal reasoning, including their method of statutory interpretation as applied to authorizing statutes and regulations. For example, did the Justice's method of statutory interpretation suggest a "purposive" approach attempting to fit any textual ambiguities with respect to the overarching purpose of the law(s) or regulatory scheme? Similarly, did the Justice take a narrow or broad reading of the statute, and what effects does a broad or narrow reading have on the an agency's discretionary and regulatory authority? This chapter will also measure the Justices' use of legislative history and track the number of times each Justice sided with or overruled the agency action in question and whether and why their decisions empowered or constrained the agency's regulatory powers/discretion.

Chapter 8 will place themes from the opinions reviewed within the context of Rohr's method of how and why to ascertain regime values through the courts. In other words, the cases are analyzed with respect to the dialectic, pertinent, institutional, and concrete aspects of the Court's decisions with a focus on Scalia and Breyer to better describe how the descriptive factors identified in chapter 7 are actualized and relevant for public administrators. Using Rohr's lens to further evaluate themes identified for each Justice will help provide meaning to the cases under review by highlighting disagreements (dialectic), address the conflict of administrative and democratic values as embodied through different types of agency discretion (pertinent), and potential long term effects of their decisions (institutional and concrete) on the courts and public administrators generally. The book closes by offering conclusions of Scalia's and Breyer's administrative law jurisprudence as it relates to public administration theory and practice. These findings are tied back to Chapter 1 to discuss how each Justices' method of legal reasoning for the cases reviewed align, or contrast with Friedrich and Finer's position regarding administrative discretion and includes lessons learned and ideas for additional research and further study.

---

[1]In *Chevron U.S.A.* v. *Natural Resources Defense Council Inc.*, 467 U.S. 837 (1984), the Court ruled that judicial deference to administrative agencies is warranted so long as the agency action gives effect to any unambiguously expressed intent of Congress. If the statute is ambiguous with respect to the specific question, the court should defer to the agency interpretation so long as that interpretation is a reasonable construction of the statute. This process is sometimes referred to as the "Chevron two-step".

[2]In *Skidmore v. Swift & Co.* 323 U.S. 134 (1944), the Court put forth a vague rule which stated the Judiciary should defer to agency interpretations of law to the extent that the agency interpretation is persuasive.

[3]For example, during Justice Scalia's nomination hearing he summarized the courts role in administrative law by saying, "all the courts are there for is to see whether the agency has followed the proper procedures, which is critically important, and whether in the final judgment the agency reaches, the agency has been within the bounds of reason". In addition, Justice Scalia's law review article, "Judicial Deference to Administrative Interpretations of Law", explains his general position that the courts should defer to agencies in most instances (1989).

[4]Other cases are interjected throughout the book to augment judicial themes found in the legal cases reviewed. For example, prior cases that are relevant, establish precedent, or are cited to support or distinguish opinions under review.

CHAPTER 2

Legal Reasoning of Breyer and Scalia

> We ask, not what [the author] meant, but what those words would mean in the mouth of a normal speaker of English, using them in the circumstances in which they were used…
>
> —Oliver Wendell Holmes, the Theory of Legal Interpretation

JUDICIAL PHILOSOPHY

To state it mildly, Justice Scalia and Breyer are considered near opposites in their approach to their role as Judge. For starters, Justice Scalia's and Breyer's Martin Quinn scores— the tool most often used to assess the ideological leanings of a Judge—are near opposites. Using this measure, Justice Breyer fits solidly within the liberal wing of the Court, and Justice Scalia is second only to Justice Thomas as the most conservative sitting Justice. In addition to their ideological differences, their overall approach to legal reasoning, constitutional and statutory interpretation as briefly outlined in chapter 1 shows they are also at odds. Both Justices agree with this assessment and have even debated with one another in public forums in defense of their stated judicial methods. Next is a look each of the Justices' professional experience along with a review of the literature showing their methods and styles of jurisprudence with a focus on writings describing their approach towards judicial review and administrative discretion.

Justice Scalia

Justice Scalia's background includes time spent teaching administrative law as a Professor of Law at the University of Virginia from 1967-

1971, University of Chicago from 1977-1982, and as a Visiting Professor of Law at the University of Georgetown and Stanford University. He was a co-founder and former editor of Regulation (a bimonthly and politically conservative magazine that analyzes government regulations and policy), and chair of the American Bar Association's Administrative Law Section from 1981-82. Justice Scalia was appointed by President Nixon as the third chair of the Administrative Conference of the United States—the purpose of which was to conduct studies and make recommendations to administrative agencies and all three branches of government regarding the efficiency, adequacy, and fairness of administrative procedures. The Administrative Conference was temporarily disbanded in 1995, but has since been reinstated as of 2010.[5] Justice Scalia has practical experience from the executive branch having worked as the Assistant Attorney General for the Justice Department's Office of Legal Counsel 1974-76, and serving four years as a Judge for the D.C. Circuit Court of Appeals prior to his arrival to the Supreme Court in 1986. Justice Scalia has published articles on administrative law and has been willing to express his legal views in different forums, including conferences, interviews, and various speaking engagements, including public debates/discussions with Justice Breyer.

Scalia has attracted the attention of many academic and legal scholars throughout his time spent on the Supreme Court. As political scientist James Staab points out, there is a "cottage industry of scholarship" directed towards Scalia that ranges from studying his charisma and writing abilities, his bold approach towards decision making, and his intellectual capabilities (2006, XV). According to Biskupic's biography of Scalia (2009), "Justice Scalia is the subject of more law journals than any other sitting Justice" (276). The dense amount of academic, editorial, and media attention given to Justice Scalia can partly be explained by one of the themes that comes out of the literature, namely that Justice Scalia has a penchant for witty remarks, catch-phrases, and sarcastic humor along with a no-holds barred approach to his legal reasoning that he puts on full display in both his legal opinions and public speaking engagements, making him an interesting subject for academic study.

According to Rossum (2005), Justice Scalia has "emerged as the Court's most outspoken, high-profile, and personally colorful member"

(2). This sentiment is echoed by Northwestern Law Professor Jerry Goldman, who quipped, "on a bench lined with solemn gray figures who often sit as silently as pigeons on a railing, Scalia stands out like a talking parrot" (Rossum 2005, Oyez 2011). More importantly, Justice Scalia's self purported adherence to textualism, originalism, and legal formalism (discussed more later on in this chapter) provides those who study Justice Scalia's opinions a fairly straight forward method to test and examine the extent to which Justice Scalia's theory meets practice, thus inviting academic attention to his jurisprudence.

After reviewing many law journals and academic articles pertaining to Justice Scalia's jurisprudence, the dominant themes were not central to the topic of judicial review of administrative discretion. Rather, the literature is focused on Justice Scalia's "style" of jurisprudence, including research assessing his conservatism, consistent (or inconsistent) application of statutory and constitutional interpretation, and his formal approach to rules and bright line tests. Research has also been focused on Justice Scalia's approach to more high profile cases such as free speech, affirmative action, religion, abortion, gun control, and homosexuality as well as his inability to create a consistent conservative bloc on the Supreme Court (Rossum 1999, 2005; Smith 1993).

That being said, there have been some comparisons between Justice Frankfurter and Justice Scalia's administrative law jurisprudence—given their shared background as administrative law professors—attempting to decipher any differences and similarities shared between the two men. For example, some scholars assessed Justice Scalia's early-years' jurisprudence on the larger topic of administrative law as resembling Frankfurter's influence under the Legal Process School (Brisbin 1997; Edelman 1991), which includes an emphasis or need for "hard look" judicial review on administrative agencies (Sunstein 1984; White 1978). As part of the Legal Process school, some have categorized Justice Scalia's early administrative law jurisprudence as embodying a "reasoned elaboration" philosophy shared by some of the Harvard Law faculty (i.e., Lon Fuller, Louis Jaffe, and Albert Sacks) that Justice Scalia studied under during his time spent in law school. However, Staab's (2006) more recent work explains how Justice Scalia's brand of conservatism and political leanings do not resemble the Legal Process School at all, but instead closely mirrors Alexander Hamilton's approach to governance. In other words, Staab makes the case that Scalia's administrative law jurisprudence is significantly influenced by his preference for a strong executive branch. However, the predominant theme emanating from the literature is that Scalia's judicial philosophy most resembles formalism, but scholars disagree regarding the extent to which Justice Scalia adheres to this method.

Scalia's critics disagree with his method of legal reasoning and constitutional and statutory interpretation from a theoretical and practical perspective and many challenge the extent to which Scalia's decisions are consistent with the judicial positions he claims to uphold. Some critics question whether Scalia is merely attempting to pursue a politically conservative agenda from the bench. For example, Merkel (2009) claims Scalia's originalist approach is a "hollow sham", and that Scalia's brand of originalism does not guard against an overly active judiciary any more-so than other methods of constitutional interpretation. Posner (2006) points out that Scalia's originalism offers no better protection to judicial arbitrariness as compared to the "Living Constitution" (which Breyer endorses), or any other method. Similarly, Straus (2008) argues that Scalia's formalistic view concerning the rule of law fails to account for the very nature of rules which, "like many other things in the world, are most often the product—the ongoing, unfinished product—of evolution" (1). Others scholars have taken issue with substantive arguments put forth by Scalia regarding administrative discretion. For example, Beermann (2010) argues that Scalia's overly broad use of judicial deference to administrative agencies frustrates Congress's intent by allowing agencies to operate essentially unchecked.

In short, there is no doubt that Scalia's jurisprudence has both fervent followers and resolute opposition. His jurisprudence is very easily described as "conservative" from a political perspective given his opinions on topics such as personal and minority rights, executive branch powers, rights of property owners (Baugh 1989; Brisbin 1990; Kanner 1990; King 1988; Moore and Fields 1988; Nagareda 1987; Rubin and Melone 1988; Wyszynski 1989) as well as more recent rulings and discussions regarding the second amendment, abortion, and religion. Reviews of Scalia's administrative law jurisprudence are oftentimes veiled behind these larger and more visible issues.

Justice Breyer

Prior to Breyer's arrival on the Court, he was already credited as having made substantial contributions to administrative doctrine, theory, and reform. Breyer's contributions to the field of administrative law derive from his published work as law professor, casebook editor and author as well as his extensive practical experience dealing with administrative law matters. Breyer was counsel to the Senate Judiciary Committee and member of the Administrative Conference of the United States. Notably, as part of the Senate Judiciary Committee, Breyer was a central figure in deregulating the airlines and was also a member of the first ever U.S. Sentencing Commission—the same commission that was challenged on Constitutional grounds in the Supreme Court case *Mistretta v. United States* - 488 U.S. 361 (1989).[6]

Breyer received his LL.B. from Harvard Law School and was Special Assistant to the Assistant U.S. Attorney General for Antitrust from 1965–1967. Breyer was the Assistant Special Prosecutor of the Watergate Special Prosecution Force in 1973 and was Professor of Law, and Lecturer at Harvard Law School, 1967–1994, Professor at the Harvard University Kennedy School of Government, 1977–1980, and a Visiting Professor at the College of Law, Sydney, Australia and at the University of Rome. From 1980–1990, Breyer served as a Judge of the United States Court of Appeals for the First Circuit, and as its Chief Judge, 1990–1994. Breyer arrived on the High Court in 1994 and has published articles on administrative law and has been willing to express his legal views in different forums, including conferences, interviews, and various speaking engagements.

Breyer is considered by many in the legal community as a "pragmatist" and whose jurisprudence most closely resembles aspects of both the legal realism and legal process school of thought (Joyce 1996; Kersch 2003; Posner 2006; Sunstein 2006). Kersch (2003) has likened his jurisprudence to that of Hart, Sacks, and Wechsler who are all pioneers in the legal process school. Federal Circuit Judge Richard Posner (2006) points out that Breyer calls for the "reasoned elaboration" approach and "hard look" approach of judicial review on administrative agencies which falls neatly in line with the legal process school. However, according to Kersch (2006), although Breyer is ultimately a product of legal realism, he embodies many types of legal scholarship including a commitment to the protection of civil rights and the changing needs of society. Moreover, Kersch notes that Breyer views American governance as evolving within a larger global context and generally prefers to defer to the expertise of other branches. Eskridge and Baer's (2008) quantitative study of Supreme Court cases from 1984-2005 supports Kersch's description by charting Breyer's overall rate of deference to agency actions between 64.9 and 79.5 percent of the time depending on the ideological stance of the agency action in question.[7]

Proponents of Breyer's judicial approach describe him as technological judge with substantive legal skills (Silverstein and Haltom 1996), and others note he serves as a moderate, with technical skills, measured analysis and a careful and pragmatic approach to constitutional interpretation (Joyce 1996, Pierce 1995, Sunstein 2006). Lubbers (1995) describes Breyer's interest in administrative law and public administration by describing him as a common-sense government reformer not only inside, also outside of the courtroom. Pierce (1995) describes Justice Breyer's early years as an intentionalist, pragmatist, and empiricist. Sunstein also regards him as a pragmatist and notes that Breyer's approach to judicial review of administrative discretion falls under Ely's general legal theory, which calls for "taking an aggressive role in some areas in order to protect democratic governance" (2006, 7). Virtually all the literature reviewed agrees with Breyer's own self-assessment that he seems to take a purposive approach in searching for the reasonable legislator's intent while keeping a watchful eye on the potential consequences of his decisions.

In response to Breyer's approach, some have criticized the amount of judicial review his theoretical accounting may affect the relationship between the Court and administrative agencies. For example, according to Posner, Breyer's call for judges to search for what the "reasonable legislator" would want as a way to guide judicial decision making, "sounds more like a method of maximizing the judge's discretion in statutory interpretation" (2006, 1711). Posner (2006) also criticizes Breyer's attempt to ground his notion of "active liberty" as a means of promoting democracy given the republican structure of US government. Sunstein (2006) and Posner (2006) deride Breyer's purposive approach of statutory interpretation by pointing out that it fails to recognize competing legislative purposes as well as potential legislative compromises respectively. For example, it could be the case there are competing views on the purpose of the legislation and by searching for a single legislative purpose to resolve ambiguities could give those who supported the statute more credit and influence than what the legislative process actually afforded. In other words, legislation is largely the product of compromise and to ignore this aspect of the legislative process is actually undemocratic. Kersche (2003) questions the benefits of Breyer's method of constitutional interpretation by noting that Breyer's "progressively inflected, purposive legal process approach" is equally likely to uphold his concept of "active liberty" as would be an "originalist" approach embodied by Justice Thomas or Scalia (780).

Scalia's Formalism

A brief explanation of legal formalism is in order given the literature has placed Justice Scalia's jurisprudence as most resembling this judicial philosophy. For starters, Justice Scalia would agree with the literature's assessment of his legal reasoning as he has written about his formal approach to law, most notably in an article he wrote in 1989 titled, "The Rule of Law as a Law of Rules" where he goes to great length explaining the virtue of formalistic rules and the risks associated with active Judges—or as Horowitz (1977) phrased it, the dangers of a "jurocracy." Lawrence Solum (2005) describes formalism as derived from a set of principles that endorse the following themes:

- The judiciary interprets law, but does not create law;
- Legal rules constrain what legal actors may lawfully do;
- There is a difference between following the law and doing what you think is best;
- Judges should decide cases in accord with the text of the applicable constitutional or statutory provision, or with the holding of controlling precedents.

According to the literature, the method of interpretation that Justice Scalia uses to interpret statutes is called "textualism," whereby interpretation turns on the plain meaning of the text and not what the legislators intended or what the judge thinks the law ought to say.

Justice Scalia purports to interpret the Constitution by searching for the original meaning of the text and not what the draftsmen intended (Scalia 1997, 38). Originalism carries an added nuance that the Constitution should be viewed from its original meaning, and not its current meaning, hence the term originalism. The shorthand term used hereafter to describe both of these methods is called "literalist."[8]

The literalist approach to interpretation is formalistic in that it seeks to limit the role of the judiciary and to derive meaning from the text of the Constitution, statutes, agency rules, regulations, and precedents, with less emphasis on consequence, legislative history, or legislative intention. According to Nelson (2005), the most common way of distinguishing literalism from its principal judicial rival, "intentionalism" (a label associated with Breyer discussed in the next section) is that intentionalists try to enforce the subjective intent of the enacting legislature, while literalists care only about the objective meaning of the statutory text (348). Said another way, formalism (and literalism) insists that Judges interpret what the law says, and not what the law should say (Cooper 2000). Justice Scalia has made clear that his approach towards constitutional and statutory interpretation falls neatly within the literalist tradition. For Justice Scalia, to be a literalist in good standing,

> "One need not be too dull to perceive the broader social purposes that a statute is designed, or could be designed, to serve; or too hidebound to realize that new times require new laws. One need only hold the belief that judges have no authority to pursue those broader purposes or write those new laws." (1988, 23)

According to Horwitz (1977) the history and development of legal formalism took root during the founding period and reached its height in the United States from approximately 1880 to early 1900's. Formalism continues to have many critics in both the academic and legal communities (Hart 1961; Horwitz 1957, 1977; Llewellyn 1962; Unger 1983; Kennedy 1973; Strauss1987; Tushnet 1985) who argue this judicial philosophy is too simple for complex legal questions and does not describe how decisions are actually made. Yet, there are others who continue to endorse a formalist approach to some extent, including sitting Supreme Court Justices Alito, Roberts, and Thomas. Legal scholar Frederick Schauer has argued that formalism is not properly understood by many critics and, "once we disentangle and examine the various strands of formalism and recognize the way in which formalism, rules, and language are conceptually intertwined, it turns out that there is something, indeed much, to be said for decision according to rule—and therefore for formalism" (1988, 510).

Breyer's Legal Realism

Legal formalism lost favor as a competing theory developed to challenge legal formalism, called legal realism. The legal realist school of thought challenged the underlying principles of legal formalism and put forth a new set of principles that claimed legal decisions are in fact non-rational and influenced by the judge's preferences and values. More importantly, legal realists believe it was right for Judges to create law and not blindly follow rules without regard for consequence or the particulars of the case at hand. Justice Breyer and other legal realists often describe formalism as "mechanical jurisprudence" given it may lead a judge to adhere to impractical rules that result in awkward or outlandish results that are clearly out of step with the intent of the legislature.

Supreme Court Justice Oliver Wendell Holmes Jr., a leading proponent of legal realism, derided formalism when he wrote, "…to believe a judge could neutrally apply well established legal rules to any or all cases was to ignore the human element of judging and the unique facts of every case" (Cooper 2000, 58-59). Following Holmes, other scholars in the legal realism movement such as Roscoe Pound, Jerome Frank, and Glendon Schubert outlined the following tenets regarding legal realism:

- Legal decisions are not rational;
- Judges have preferences and values that affect their decisions;
- Judges' decisions, especially on multi-member appellate courts, are affected by small group dynamics found in any collegial body;
- Strict legal principles should be eschewed in legal decision making; rather the judge is tasked with understanding the

> particular facts of a case and arriving at a decision that addresses those specific facts (Cooper 59).

A strand of legal realism as employed by some legal realist followers—including Breyer, and the credited founder of legal realism Oliver Wendell Holmes—is the concept of intentionalism. Intentionalism is a label used to describe Justices who strive to understand the legislative intent or what a reasonable legislator would have thought as a primary method to guide decisions. Although the method of intentionalism is not limited to the legal realism school of thought, it is noted here because it is commonly associated with Breyer and legal realism, as legal realism emphasizes the judge's role in pursuit of justice and consequences through the use of their own legal discernment apart from any predetermined rules. Although legal realism is considered to have taken root during the 1920 -30's, traces of intentionalism can be found as far back as antiquity.

For example, the intentionalist approach resembles a description of law put forth by Thrasymachus—a character in Plato's *Republic*—who explained that justice as applied through government is nothing more than the interest of the stronger. Given the direct democracy in power at the time Plato was writing, stronger would be associated with the people's will. Thus, it follows the character Thrasymachus would expect courts charged with interpreting the law to predominantly defer to the will of the people as legislators. In the same vein, Justice Holmes conveyed a similar notion of deferring to the will of the people (through laws) in a dissent he authored for the Supreme Court stating, "It is settled by various decisions of this court that state constitutions and state laws may regulate life in many ways which we, as legislators, might think as injudicious, or, if you like, as tyrannical…" (*Lochner v. New York*, 198 U.S. 75 (1905). Similarly, Breyer employs the intentionalist approach on the topic of judicial review of administrative agencies when he writes that a judge should,

> "…ask whether, given the statutory aims and circumstances, a hypothetical member [i.e., a reasonable member of Congress] would likely have wanted judicial deference in this situation," or, contrariwise, would have wanted to decide the question for himself". (2005, 106)

Note, the question for Breyer as articulated here is whether Congress wanted for itself or the courts to decide the matter, but no discussion on whether Congress may have wanted the agency to resolve the statutory ambiguity. This classical notion of legislative power and democracy is also a theme that runs throughout Justice Breyer's (2005) book, *Active Liberty: Interpreting our Democratic Constitution*, which argues for the "Lliving Constitution" method of jurisprudence which empowers judges to assess the values of the Constitution in relation to the ever changing times and as a way to promote democratic values.

Breyer best exemplifies his regard for intent and legal realism when he contrasts his position to that of Scalia's by asking, "why would the framers have preferred (1) a system of interpretation that relies heavily on linguistic canons to (2) a system that seeks more directly to find the *intent* of the legislators who enacted the stature?" (emphasis added 2005, 117) Breyer goes on to say, "originalists cannot access the intent of the framers and the Constitution does not specify what method one should use to interpret text" (2005, 117), once again placing emphasis on intention and consequence, thus necessitating judgment that more closely resembles legal realism than any other method of jurisprudence.

Although the purpose of this book is not intended to solve the long-standing and continuing debate of whether legal formalism or legal realism is most appropriate or misguided, the literature has focused on the extent to which both Justices apply their stated philosophies in practice, thus it is important to understand their general approach to law for the purposes of this research project. Specifically, understanding formalism, legal realism, and both of their methods towards constitutional and statutory interpretation helps to better assess and compare their administrative law jurisprudence and how it can be used to inform public administration.

Rohr's Regime Values

As briefly mentioned in chapter 1, Rohr's regime values are used herein to help focus and understand Justice Scalia's and Breyer's administrative law jurisprudence as it relates to public administration theory and practice. Rohr's 1998 book, *Public Service, Ethics, and*

Constitutional Practice designates a chapter in discussing how the academy should teach ethics to students of public administration. Rohr argues that public administration ethics should be grounded in the Constitution instead of the history of political philosophy and humanistic psychology (1998, 20). Rohr's decision to focus on the Constitution is partly because the demand of teaching the entire history of political philosophy is unreasonable for many public administration programs and a humanistic psychology approach to ethics does not take into account the institutional role of governance and the demands of the career public administrator. However, it is the substantive arguments made in favor of basing ethics on the Constitution and the courts, discussed next, which is most relevant for the purposes of this book.

For Rohr, the decision of an individual to swear an oath to the Constitution prior to assuming one's position in the administrative state pre-supposes that the individual has already answered the question of whether or not the regime values of the administrative state are in tune with one's own values. From this premise, Rohr argues that it is more appropriate for the academy to focus on teaching the lesser issues of how can one promote the values of the regime, as opposed to the larger political philosophy question of, is the regime just? (1998, 22). By focusing on the lesser and more practical approach towards ethics, Rohr argues that the question then becomes how to discern what the American regime values are and how public administrators should seek to apply them.

The method put forth by Rohr to answer these questions is to study and teach major Supreme Court decisions regarding salient American values such as freedom, property, and equality (1998, 24). This project attempts to incorporate that method by focusing on cases whereby Justice Scalia and Breyer are forced to outline those values to some extent for public administrators, as they formulate opinions regarding whether or not agency actions, decisions, and interpretations of authorizing legislation conflict or support salient constitutional values. In other words, by reviewing cases that focus on judicial review of administrative discretion, an interested public administrator may find benefit from observing how these Justices' varied approaches go about applying the Constitution to 21st century demands of public administration. Of course, it is important for public administrators to try and understand how to apply legal and constitutional norms within their sphere of autonomy as administrative decisions affect not only the day to day operations of government, but also the very principles and ideals of what constitutes a legitimate government. For Rohr, reviewing Supreme Court decisions is an excellent way to go about ascertaining the country's guiding principles because the decisions of the Supreme Court are institutional, dialectic, concrete, and pertinent. These four pillars are described next.

Institutional

By institutional, Rohr means that the Supreme Court weighs past precedents and historic values developed over time while attempting to answer new constitutional questions. Rohr writes, "the nature of the judicial process involves tension between past and present and courts frequently solve current issues with a creative interpretation of a familiar principle" (1998, 25). For Rohr, it is important for public administrators attempting to identify values to distinguish "stable principles" from "passing whims" (1998, 25). Given every Justice is limited to the vision of his or her time in history, the institutional values of the Court help paint a broader picture towards understanding the historic values that are developed over many years (1998, 25).

Dialectic

Rohr describes the Court as dialectic given the majority, concurring, and dissenting opinions cover both sides of legal arguments allowing the bureaucrat to critically assess important questions in different ways. Unlike the executive and legislative branches of government, the Supreme Court must document the reasoning behind their decisions which allows public administrators a window to study well reasoned legal arguments in a formal context (1998, 26). Rohr also values dissenting opinions when he writes that, "vigorous dissents can at times force the majority of the Court to provide better reasons for its decision that it would have offered if there had been no challenge" (1998, 26-27). Moreover, public confidence is increased when serious argument replaces simple assertions (1998, 27). Finally, oftentimes the majority, concurring, and dissenting opinions point out weaknesses in the opposing view, which over time may further instruct or refine later Court opinions.

Concrete

Rohr explains that Supreme Court decisions are also concrete given the Court is the final decision maker and the results of their decisions are binding. Unlike political philosophers who are free to engage in theoretical arguments without restraint, the Court must eventually render a final decision to be put in practice, thus fusing theory and practice into public policy (1998, 27). For Rohr, the concreteness of judicial decisions helps bureaucrats to assess values from a practical perspective, instead of purely theoretical. In other words, judicial decisions can help public administrators reflect upon values such as freedom, property, and equality, when these broad concepts are refined through Supreme Court opinions that are wrestling with real life practical scenarios and legal questions.

Pertinent

Rohr makes the point that significant and controversial issues typically make their way to the Supreme Court. For example, watershed legal issues such as slavery, constitutionality of federal income tax, and government regulation of industry have all reached the High Court. Rohr gives the example that the Watergate scandal was headline news for essentially 2 years—evidencing this was a significant case challenging American morals and political values—and the fact that all parties and the public quickly turned to the Court, supports the notion that the Court is expected to serve as the nation's "...arbiters of values" (28). Regarding public administration, Rohr writes, "Supreme Court opinions are especially and, perhaps, even uniquely suitable for the bureaucrat seeking enlightenment on the meaning of American values" (28). Given the Supreme Court also sets the standards by which lower courts are expected to follow serves as more reason to begin the search for pertinent cases that affect public administration at the highest level of the Judicial Branch.

---

[5]Justice Breyer and Scalia were the only Supreme Court Justices asked to speak to the House Judiciary committee regarding the role and utility of the Administrative Conference. Given Scalia was a former Chair and Breyer a member of the Administrative Conference, it is not surprising both Justices advocated for Congress to reinstate and support the mission of the Administrative Conference during the hearing.

[6]Interestingly for this project, Justice Scalia authored a lone dissent in this case arguing that the commission was unconstitutional and violated the non-delegation doctrine and the separation of powers.

[7]Eskridge and Baer point out their quantitative analysis is determined by agencies winning cases and may not account for when the Court invokes deference to the agency, but the agency position still does not win the case because of some other legal reason. Similarly, when the Court does not rule in favor of the agency, the agency interpretation might still prevail in the overall opinion. The qualitative analysis for this project will help answer what factors and circumstances came into play regarding judicial review of administrative discretion and accurately account whether siding with the agency constrained or enabled administrative discretion.

[8]The shorthand term "literalist" in place of textualism and originalism is used throughout for this project and is a term that has been adopted by others including Justice Breyer (2005, 116).

CHAPTER 3

SEC, FDA, and FCC Agency Actions

> The statute's language, then, permits the agency to choose remedies consistent with its basic purpose—the overall protection of public health.
>
> —Justice Breyer, *FDA v. Brown & Williamson Tobacco Corporation*

CASE REVIEWS

This chapter begins the legal case briefings for Breyer and Scalia involving actions taken by the Food and Drug Administration (FDA), the Securities and Exchange Commission (SEC), and 3 cases involving the Federal Communications Commission (FCC). These cases address agency discretion in a myriad of ways, including agency notice-and-comment rulemaking, adjudication, and interpretive/substantive rules.

The first case reviewed stems from an opinion Scalia wrote concurring in part and dissenting in part for *United States v. O'Hagan* 521 U.S. 642 (1997) (hereafter *O'Hagan*) questioning whether a substantive rule promulgated by the SEC went beyond the agency's rulemaking powers. The next case discussed comes from Breyer's dissenting opinion in the controversial 5-4 decision whereby the Court ruled in *Food and Drug Administration v. Brown & Williamson Tobacco Corporation* 529 U.S. 120 (2000) (hereafter *Brown*) the FDA had no authority under statute to regulate tobacco. The FCC cases under review include *FCC v. Fox Television Stations Inc.*, 556 U.S. 502 (2009) (hereafter *Fox Television Inc.*) whereby Scalia authors the majority opinion and Breyer the dissent, regarding whether the agency's position on the legality of fleeting expletives was "arbitrary and capricious" under the APA. The next case reviewed in this chapter

Talk America Inc., v. Michigan Bell Telephone Co., 564 U.S. (2011) (hereafter *Talk America Inc.*) stems from a concurring opinion authored by Scalia discussing the normative implications of courts deferring to agency interpretations of their own ambiguous regulations, and how that practice may affect the constitutional separation of powers. This chapter ends with a review of *City of Arlington, Texas v. Federal Communications Commission* (hereafter *City of Arlington*) challenging the outer-boundaries of *Chevron* deference as Scalia writes for the majority and Breyer writes a separate opinion to deviate his position from Scalia's on judicial review of administrative discretion. It is noteworthy that Breyer and Scalia voted with opposite sides of the Court for 3 of the 5 cases reviewed in this chapter. Also, Breyer deferred to the agency in 4 of the 5 cases, and Scalia deferred in 3 cases and deferred in part for 1 case.

O'Hagan

The first case *O'Hagan* involves the Securities and Exchange Commission (SEC) and whether or not a rule the agency passed defining insider trading to forbid security trading of nonpublic information of a tender offer (i.e., a public offer to buy stock from shareholders at a price substantively higher than market value at a specific time), was within the agency's discretionary rulemaking power. In this case, Grand Metropolitan PLC hired a law firm to assist in preparations to make a tender offer to purchase Pillsbury Company stock. One of the attorneys (O'Hagan) not assigned to the case, nevertheless heard about the potential tender offer and purchased a large amount of Pillsbury stock options without telling the law firm. O'Hagan sold his new stock options for a $4.3 million profit as soon as the tender offer was made public. The SEC indicted O'Hagan on 57 counts of fraud for misappropriating nonpublic information and defrauding the law firm and the client (i.e., investor, Grand metropolitan PLC). The jury convicted O'Hagan on all counts, but the US Court of Appeals for the 8th Circuit reversed by narrowing the SEC's reach, explaining the fraud rules only pertain to security traders who violate their own company. Moreover, the 8th Circuit held that the SEC overreached their rulemaking authority by promulgating a rule prohibiting security trading with foreknowledge of a tender offer without a fiduciary duty requirement.

The Court was facing two legal questions. First, is a person, who trades in securities for personal profit, using confidential information misappropriated, in breach of a fiduciary duty to the source of the information guilty of violating SEC's rules 10(b) and Rule 10b–5? The distinction underlying this question is whether "source of information" (as opposed to employer) can be made to fit the statute. The second question is the more central question for the purposes for this project as it focuses on whether the SEC exceeded its rulemaking authority by adopting Rule 14e–3(a), which forbids trading on undisclosed information in the tender offer setting, even in the absence of a duty to disclose. The 8th Circuit framed the question succinctly through their opinion holding that the authorizing statute allows the SEC to identify and regulate fraudulent acts, but the agency is not authorized to create a unique definition of fraud.

Justice Ginsburg wrote the 6-3 majority opinion reversing the 8th Circuit on both questions. Breyer joined the majority opinion and Scalia wrote a separate opinion concurring in part and dissenting in part. Thomas wrote a dissenting opinion joined by Rehnquist. The first question regarding respondent's liability under the authorizing statute is not particularly germane to this project. With that in mind, suffice it to say the Court held, and Scalia and Breyer agreed, that O'Hagan was liable under the statute and that liability does not hinge exclusively on a breach of duty owed to a purchaser or seller of securities.

Before moving to the more central question for this project, it is worth noting a point raised in Thomas's dissent in regards to the question of liability as it relates to Scalia's and Breyer's method of statutory interpretation. Namely, Thomas explains the Court takes a "purposive" approach to interpreting the statute. According to Thomas, the majority "...reaches too far in that, regardless of the overarching purpose of the securities laws, it is not illegal to run afoul of the 'purpose' of a statute, only its letter" (689). In other words, according to Thomas, the majority opinion is looking beyond the statutory text to support the agency regulation. A purpose approach fits nicely with Breyer, but one would expect Scalia to counter this criticism given his self-purported view of literalism and stated unwillingness to search for statutory purpose. Yet, Scalia's separate concurring/dissenting opinion does not address this point at all. Similarly, Thomas takes up another point central to Scalia's stated jurisprudence regarding separation of powers when he explains that the Court's reading of the authorizing statute in question is overly broad for a criminal statute, especially given this open ended reading allows an independent agency (SEC) to define fraud. Given Scalia's dissent in *Mistretta (*discussed more in Thomas's dissent below*)*, the author would have expected Scalia to take up this argument as well, but he does not.

Moving now to the rulemaking question, Ginsburg's majority opinion addresses whether the agency exceeded its rulemaking authority by first citing the authorizing statute which reads:

> It shall be unlawful for any person . . . to engage in any fraudulent, deceptive, or manipulative acts or practices, in connection with any tender offer . . . . The [SEC]shall, for the purposes of this subsection, by rules and regulations define, and prescribe means reasonably designed to prevent, such acts and practices as are fraudulent, deceptive, or manipulative. (15 U. S. C. § 78n(e))

The questionable part of the agency rule in relation to the above statute is whether a nondisclosure can be categorized as fraud if there is no fiduciary duty on part of the actor. Ginsburg cites numerous cases that support the position it is the responsibility of traders to abstain or disclose, without regard to whether the trader owes a pre-existing fiduciary duty. Namely, Ginsburg relies on the precedent set in *Schreiber v. Burlington Northern, Inc.,* 472 U. S. 11 (1985) which discusses the SEC rule in question by holding in part, "rulemaking authorization gives the Commission 'latitude'" (673). Ginsburg continues by explaining Congress has specifically authorized legislative powers to the SEC and thus the Court should defer to the agency according to *Chevron* unless the actions are arbitrary, capricious, or manifestly contrary to the statute. Ginsburg holds that the rule is valid in part because of the agency explanation accompanying the rule that details the purpose and reasoning behind the rule. For Ginsburg, the agency essentially justified the rule as a means necessary and proper to assure the efficacy of the authorizing statute.

Ginsburg also seems to take a pragmatic approach to the laws implementation by drawing attention to the likelihood that multiple people, such as lawyers, investment bankers, and accountants who may help structure large stockholder deals could potentially have foreknowledge of non-public information without having a fiduciary responsibility. For Ginsburg, it makes sense for the agency to promulgate rules to prevent and deter such instances of fraud given the temptation to act on such knowledge carries significant financial motivation. In other words, the majority opinion goes beyond the authorizing statute to some degree and gives weight to the agency's attempt to regulate a very possible, perhaps even commonplace occurrence, which left unchecked can disturb market values and fairness to shareholders. This aspect of the majority opinion seems reminiscent of Breyer's calling for the courts to "make democracy work." In short, the majority held that the agency's "disclose or abstain from trading" provision (which does not require a breach of fiduciary duty) is a "means reasonably designed to prevent" fraudulent trading on material, nonpublic information in the tender offer context.

Thomas's dissent begins by arguing the majority's reading of the authorizing statutory text is incorrect. Thomas agrees with the 8th Circuits reading which states the statute allows for the SEC to "identify and regulate those acts and practices" that meet the legal definition of "fraudulent," but does not allow the agency to "redefine the term." Thomas also takes issue with the agency's rulemaking powers from a constitutional perspective. Using an analogy, Thomas notes a law that states, "it shall be unlawful to do 'X', however 'X' shall be defined by an independent agency," offers no "intelligible principle" to help guide an agency's use of discretion. For Thomas, such an expansive delegation of power from Congress to the agency could invoke the court's rarely used non-delegation doctrine which states one agency cannot delegate powers to another agency that the agency itself is constitutionally responsible for implementing. Interestingly, the "intelligible principle" mentioned by Thomas was also discussed in the *Mistretta* case, whereby Scalia wrote a lone dissent explaining the United States Sentencing Committee that established sentencing guidelines violated the separation of powers and the non-delegation doctrine. In that case, Scalia explained the independent agency was essentially making laws that were laden with values and policies central to the work of legislators, or in his words, the commission was acting as a "...sort of Junior Varsity Congress." It is surprising to find that Scalia does not take up this argument pointed out by Thomas given the SEC is also an independent agency, and similar to the *Mistretta* case which questioned how to categorize criminal sentencing penalties, the case here is an independent agency developing the meaning of a criminal statute by defining fraud.

Instead, Scalia's opinion concurring in part and dissenting in part takes issue only with the majority's opinion regarding the analysis of the respondent's convictions. Scalia begins by recognizing that when an agency has either adjudicative powers or policymaking discretion, any agency actions must align with the reasons the agency sets forth, but not necessarily for instances where the agency is simply doing what is required by law. For Scalia, the matter is simple; either the respondent violated the statute and rule, or did not. Scalia explains this is especially the case given the Court is not offering *Chevron* deference to this part of the opinion because the agency rule is just as ambiguous as the authorizing statute. Scalia describes the majority's opinion regarding the first question of liability and breach of duty as not comporting with the Court's "rule of lenity" for criminal statutes.[9] Thus, Scalia explains that a reading of the statute that employs the rule of lenity would necessarily rule in favor of respondent and not the government.

Brown

The first case review for Breyer stems from a dissent he authored in *Brown* involving the scope of FDA's regulatory power over tobacco. In 1995, the FDA published a proposed rule concerning the sale of cigarettes and smokeless tobacco to children and adolescents.[10] The FDA interpreted the authorizing legislation (Food, Drug, and Cosmetic Act (ACT)), as amended in 1938, as giving the FDA jurisdiction over the regulation of tobacco. In short, the FDA concluded that nicotine is a drug within the meaning of the Act and that cigarettes and smokeless tobacco are "combination products" (meeting the statutory term "devices") that deliver nicotine to the body. During the FDA's rulemaking proceedings, the agency went to great lengths to scientifically demonstrate the dangers of smoking in support of the eventual decision to put forth rules aimed at curbing minors' interest and potential use of cigarettes as a public safety matter. Soon after in 1996, the FDA put forth regulations regarding the promotion, labeling, and accessibility to children and adolescents for tobacco products. Specifically, the regulations took the following 10 measures:

1. prohibited the sale of cigarettes or smokeless tobacco to persons younger than 18;
2. required retailers to verify through photo identification the age of all purchasers younger than 27;
3. prohibited the sale of cigarettes in quantities smaller than 20;
4. prohibited the distribution of free samples;
5. prohibited sales through self-service displays and vending machines except in adult-only locations.
6. any print advertising must appear in black-and-white, text-only format unless the publication in which it appears is read almost exclusively by adults;
7. prohibited outdoor advertising within 1,000 feet of any public playground or school;
8. prohibited the distribution of any promotional items, such as T-shirts or hats, bearing the manufacturer's brand name;
9. prohibited a manufacturer from sponsoring any athletic, musical, artistic, or other social or cultural event using its brand name.
10. required the statement, "A Nicotine-Delivery Device for Persons 18 or Older," appear on all tobacco product packages.

Brown & Williamson Tobacco Corporation, along with other cigarette manufacturers, retailers, and advertisers, filed suit challenging the FDA's regulations. The District Court ruled that the FDA was correct in assuming jurisdiction over tobacco as a "device", but the agency does not have the discretionary power to promulgate rules specifically restricting advertising and promotion. The Court of Appeals reversed and held that Congress did not intend for the FDA to regulate tobacco products at all, answering the jurisdiction question, but not addressing whether the agency regulations exceeded their authority.

Writing for the High Court, Justice O'Connor's majority opinion affirmed the Court of Appeals in 5-4 decision holding that the FDA was wrong to issue regulations involving tobacco. Namely, the majority opinion explained that in light of the complete legislative history and actions taken by Congress over the years, that Congress never intended for the FDA or any agency to have jurisdiction over the regulation of tobacco. In addition, the authorizing legislation in question does not fit the case of tobacco because it requires that the FDA prohibit dangerous drugs or devices such as cigarettes outright, and O'Connor noted even the FDA concedes that an over arching ban on cigarettes is not a proper remedy. Despite the agency in this case attempting to promulgate rules regarding the very statute it is authorized to uphold, the majority opinion ultimately decided not to grant *Chevron* deference, and instead overturned the agency action as both not having jurisdiction, and not properly issuing rules that meet the intent of the authorizing statute, thus the agency's use of discretion in this case was determined out of bounds.

Interestingly, as part of O'Connor's support for the decision to not simply defer to the agency's interpretation of the statute, Justice O'Connor cites Breyer's academic article, "Judicial Review of Questions of Law and Policy" where Breyer offers an alternate route to judicial deference to agencies when he writes, "A court may also ask whether the legal question is an important one. Congress is more likely to have focused upon, and answered, major questions, while leaving interstitial matters to answer themselves in the course of the statute's daily administration" (1986, 38). For O'Connor, FDA's new found role in regulating cigarettes would have enormous market effects, and would thus meet Breyer's description of a "major question" that Congress is better suited to answer. Breyer addresses this point in his dissent by citing *Kent v. Dulles*, 357 U.S. 116, 129 (1958) which notes that when interpreting statutes, the courts should assume in close cases that a decision with enormous social consequences, should be made by democratically elected Members of Congress rather than by unelected agency administrators, but then quickly dismisses this notion in the following sentence stating, "if there is such a background canon of interpretation, however, I do not believe it controls the outcome here" (190). At this point, Breyer explains that an administrative agency decision as, "important, conspicuous, and controversial" as this particular action will undoubtedly invite public scrutiny and the President and Congress will necessarily give the matter attention. This sentiment echoes Breyer's books which also call for an empowered, attentive, and active democracy to pressure elected officials as a way to check government agencies.

The majority opinion (joined by Scalia), relies heavily on legislative history to discern that Congress has never intended for the FDA to have jurisdiction regarding tobacco because there have never been any specific legislation calling for the FDA to regulate the industry. Although O'Connor recognizes in her opinion that "whether the Congress that enacted the FDCA specifically intended the Act to cover tobacco products is not determinative"—thus recognizing the legislative history is not controlling for the Courts—"nonetheless the intent is certainly relevant to understanding the basis for the FDA's representations to Congress and the background against which Congress enacted subsequent tobacco-specific legislation" (146). The majority opinion goes on to make note of 4 legislative bills proposed but never adopted into law prior to 1965 as evidence the Congress at large has never been interested in the FDA regulating tobacco. To make clear of what the legislative purpose was that the Congress voted against, O'Connor quotes a sponsoring Senator who explained, "this amendment simply places smoking products under FDA jurisdiction, along with foods, drugs, and cosmetics" (147).

The majority opinion goes on to list subsequent laws passed related to tobacco that have not specifically called for FDA regulation of tobacco including the Alcohol and Drug Abuse Amendments (1983), Comprehensive Smoking Education Act (1984), and the Comprehensive Smokeless Tobacco Health Education Act (1986), none of which called for FDA to regulate tobacco to the extent in question for the Court's review. The majority opinion cites elected and agency officials' statements during various hearings and floor debates throughout the opinion to support the position that it is has been well understood that Congress has purposely reserved tobacco regulation for itself and not the FDA or any other agency.

It was interesting to see that for a majority opinion that was significantly influenced by the legislative history, along with attempts to assess the intentions of legislators over the years, including those bills that were not passed into law, that Scalia was not compelled to write a separate opinion that made clear his judgment was not dependent on the Congressional history that he claims to ignore in his jurisprudence. In contrast, Breyer (who does advocate for the use of legislative history) puts forth a dissenting opinion that takes aim at the use of legislative history (and Justice Scalia specifically) by pointing out Scalia's concurring opinion in *Sullivan v. Finkelstein*, 496 U.S. 617 (1990) where Scalia stated, "Arguments based on subsequent legislative history ... should not be taken seriously, not even in a footnote". In other words, both Justices' theoretical stance on legislative history was not only ignored, but they both actually embraced the opposite view.

Breyer's dissent calls for a much broader reading of the authorizing legislation that focuses on Congress' larger goal of protecting health. For Breyer, the focus of Congress' intent is found through the authorizing statute and not the legislative history put forth by the majority opinion. According to Breyer the statute, "requires a flexible interpretation that both permits the FDA to take into account the realities of human behavior and allows it, in appropriate cases, to choose from its arsenal of statutory remedies" (181). One of the statutory remedies that Breyer accepts is the way in which the FDA balances the safety and effects an outright ban would have on consumers. For example, Breyer agrees with the FDA's position that the agency is right to consider the possible bad effects of banning cigarettes, such as withdrawal symptoms, or the possibility of consumers purchasing stronger, more dangerous, or black-market cigarettes.

Whereas the majority opinion contends the statute itself does not allow for agency considerations of all possible bad effects in the aggregate, Breyer embraces this consequentialist approach and sees this as an available factor for agencies to consider. Breyer also finds some support for this view in the statutory text which states, "no device recall if "risk of recall" presents "a greater health risk than" no recall (178). Finally, for Breyer, the FDA was right to claim jurisdiction and apply regulations as the science supporting the dangers of smoking had continually increased over the years, reaching a threshold that simply demanded FDA attention. In this strand of Breyer's dissent, the echoes of Friedrich's position can be heard calling for technically competent bureaucrats advancing regulations that meet the demands of science and empiricism. Interestingly, Justice Breyer's dissent served as a pre-cursor to the Family Smoking Prevention and Tobacco Control Act passed in 2009 that now gives the FDA unquestionable jurisdiction to regulate tobacco.

Fox Television Stations Inc.

The next case under review, *Fox Television Stations Inc.*, reads like an intellectual heavy-weight match between Breyer and Scalia on the topic of administrative discretion as Scalia writes for the majority and Breyer the dissent for a 5-4 decision. In this case the Court was asked to determine whether the FCC's change order reversing the agency's position on the legality of fleeting expletives was "arbitrary and capricious" under the Administrative Procedure. To understand the implications of the ruling, both opinions first describe the FCC's regulatory history (interestingly, each Justice describes the regulatory historical development a bit differently) and the authorizing legislation.

Scalia begins by noting the FCC's first statutory ban on indecent broadcasts occurring in 1975 whereby the FCC declared a daytime broadcast of George Carlin's "Filthy Words" monologue as indecent. Specifically, the FCC specified:

> language that describes, in terms patently offensive as measured by contemporary community standards for the broadcast medium, sexual or excretory activities or organs, at times of the day when there is a reasonable risk that children may be in the audience. U. S. C. [§] 1464

Scalia notes the FCC clarified the reasoning behind that order by explaining each literal "description or depiction of sexual or excretory functions must be examined in context to determine whether it is patently offensive," but that "deliberate and repetitive use . . . is a requisite to a finding of indecency" for the use of "nonliteral" expletives.

The FCC used the same definition for indecency for over a decade until the singer Bono from U2 uttered the F-word during a live broadcast of the Golden Globe Awards on NBC. After which the FCC changed course and declared that a non-literal expletive use of the F- and S- words could also be indecent, even if said only once. The FCC reasoned that to allow fleeting expletives would "likely lead to more widespread use" and that technological advances have made it easy for to bleep out a "single and gratuitous use of a vulgar expletive." This background sets the stage for the case at hand which stems from 2 separate instances whereby expletives were used during a live broadcast aired by Fox Television Stations and affiliates.

In the first case, the singer Cher exclaimed during the 2002 Billboard Music Awards, "I've also had critics for the last 40 years saying that I was on my way out every year. Right. So f*** 'em." The second instance also occurred during the Billboard Music Awards (2003), whereby during the presentation of an award by Nicole Richie and Paris Hilton—stars of the Fox television series called "The Simple Life"—Ms. Hilton told Ms. Richie to "watch the bad language," and Ms. Richie proceeded to ask the audience, "Why do they even call it 'The Simple Life?' Have you ever tried to get cow s*** out of a Prada purse? It's not so f***ing simple."

In 2006 the FCC released Notices of Apparent Liability for numerous broadcasts from 2002 – 2005 which included the 2 aforementioned cases. Given the order did not impose sanctions (as previous precedent allowed for fleeting expletives) the broadcasters did not have an opportunity to challenge the indecency charges and therefore the broadcasters obtained a voluntary remand from the Court of Appeals to plead their case. On remand, the FCC did not change their position and held that the two scenarios in this case were indecent using either the prior precedent or the post-Golden Globe standard. Furthermore, the FCC explained that by allowing fleeting expletives forces viewers to take the "first blow" and would allow broadcasters to air expletives one at a time all day long. Once again, no sanctions resulted from the outcome of the remand order. Fox returned to the 2nd Circuit for review of the updated remand order and the Court of Appeals reversed the agency's orders, explaining the agency's actions were arbitrary and capricious under the APA.

Scalia's 5-4 majority opinion reversed and remanded the 2nd Circuit's opinion and upheld the FCC's position. For Scalia, the case turned on his reasoning that the courts do not require a "heightened" state of review simply because an agency reverses or changes their position. In other words, the agency does not have to show that the new position is necessarily "better" than a previous position, but only show that the new position is "reasonable". Scalia furthers this point by explaining the APA's arbitrary and capricious standards do not differentiate between initial agency actions and subsequent actions that may revise those initial actions.

The case cited by both sides as import precedent for consideration is the landmark *Motor Vehicle Manufacturers Association of United States, Inc. v. State Farm Mutual Automobile Insurance. Co.*, 463 U. S. 29 (1983) (hereafter *State Farm*)[11]. Scalia explains that *State Farm* precedent requires the courts to, "examine the relevant data and articulate a satisfactory explanation for its action." In contrast, Breyer's dissent describes *State Farm* as requiring that "an agency must provide an explanation for the agency's 'revocation' of a prior action that is more thorough than the explanation necessary when it does not act in the first instance." For Breyer, "the Court defined 'revocation,' not simply as rescinding an earlier policy, but as a reversal of the agency's former views as to the proper course" (549).

Scalia addresses Breyer's contention in a footnote saying *State Farm* "did not assert the authority of a court to demand explanation sufficient to enable it to weigh (by its own lights) the merits of the agency's change" (515). For Scalia, "the agency need not always provide a more detailed justification than what would suffice for a new policy created on a blank slate" (515). Scalia also points out that it would not be fair to require the agency to produce empirical data—as required by *State Farm* which called for a cost benefit analysis—because in this case empirical evidence is unobtainable. Scalia gives the example that one cannot expect the FCC to acquire a multiyear controlled study where some children are exposed to indecent language and others are not to then measure the effects.

An interesting point raised by the Respondents but not addressed by the dissent is whether the FCC's new order which calls for the context and consideration of all factors regarding indecency is nothing more than a "smokescreen for a standardless regime of unbridled discretion" for agencies to use in the future. To some extent this criticism carries some weight as the new order simply says the fleeting expletives may now be considered indecent depending on context, without specifically defining such contextual considerations. However, Scalia contends that this context based approach is consistent with previous court rulings and the APA does not call for anything different.

Breyer's dissent argues that the FCC's decision to change position on the "fleeting expletive" is arbitrary, capricious, and an abuse of discretion. Breyer explains that the agency failed to explain "why" it changed positions adequately and the reasoning employed by the agency for the change of position was based on factors well understood during the time the original rules were put in place. In this case, Breyer notes two specific reasons the agency view should fall: (1) the FCC did not adequately address the relation between the change it made from its prior "fleeting expletive" policy and the First-Amendment-related need to avoid censorship, and, (2) did not adequately address the financial impact of censoring (i.e., "bleeping") technology for small independent and local broadcasters and the effects the new rule would have on their willingness to broadcast live and public events in the future.

To this first point, Breyer argues that the FCC "works in the shadow" of the Constitution's first amendment and has historically made clear over the years that the agency aims to avoid encroaching on Constitutional protections of free speech. Breyer cites 5 instances whereby the FCC wrote statements explaining the agency's position on indecency—with respect to the Constitution and the Court precedent—which for Breyer shows the agency made clear the fleeting expletive policy was focused upon the need to avoid treading too close to the constitutional line. In short, Breyer expects the agency to document how the new policy change fits within the 1st Amendment concerns the agency has long debated and considered. Breyer notes in reviewing the agency orders under review, the 400 page document only includes a 28 word description on this matter stating their decision is consistent with Court precedent which left open the issue of whether a fleeting expletive could be considered indecent. For Breyer, this does not adequately show the agency considered the new policy with respect to the Constitution and warrants a remand back to the agency for further consideration of the point. Scalia addresses Breyer's call for remand with a statement just as brief as the FCC explanation Breyer criticizes, when he writes "we are unaware that we have ever before reversed an executive agency, not for violating our cases, but for failure to discuss them adequately" (526).

Breyer's second point regarding the local broadcasters was simply that the FCC did not consider how the financial costs of "bleeping" technology may affect local broadcasting. Specifically, Breyer is concerned whether smaller broadcasting companies that cannot afford the new technology will risk covering live events under the new rule. Breyer notes the importance of local broadcasts by citing 3 FCC regulations that attest to the value local broadcasts add to the communication medium and the important role these outlets have for ensuring a diversity of views on the airwaves. Breyer points out the amicus brief provided to the Court which explains the cost of the censoring and delay technology can cost as much as $100,000 to install and operate which is more some stations earn in profits for an entire year. Breyer adds that coupling this with a potential fine from the FCC of up to $325,000 for violating the new rule and it is not hard to surmise that local broadcasters may hesitate to cover live events.

Scalia's majority opinion seems to be at its lowest ebb regarding this point as he answers Breyer's criticism by speculating, "down-home local guests probably employ vulgarity less than big-city folks; and small-town stations generally cannot afford or cannot attract foul-mouthed glitteratae from Hollywood" (527). It seems reasonably safe to say there is no evidentiary support for such a position, hence why no citation was provided. Scalia's response improves slightly by inferring the FCC reserves some discretion that can benefit a local broadcaster by pointing to the FCC order which states, "it may be inequitable to hold a licensee responsible for airing offensive speech during live coverage of a public event." However, it is clear this is an inference and not necessarily evidence that the agency considered the matter as Breyer's dissent demands.

A final note on this case is especially relevant in regards to Scalia. Justice Stevens makes the charge that Scalia seems to have abandoned his non-reliance on legislative history to support his position. Stevens' criticism warrants a full citation,

> It appears that Justice Scalia has come to the view that isolated statements by members of a congressional oversight subcommittee are sufficient evidence of Congress' intent. Delving into the details of how various lawmakers 'grilled' the full slate of FCC Commissioners, Justice Scalia concludes, quite remarkably, that this encounter 'made clear Congress' wishes for stricter enforcement' and 'would seem an adequate explanation of [the FCC's] change of position'. Putting to the

> side the question whether congressional outrage is the kind of evidence sufficient to explain the Commission's decision to adopt a thinly-reasoned and unconstitutional policy, Justice Scalia's treatment of these proceedings as evidencing the intent of Congress would make even the most ardent student of legislative history blush. (542 fn3)

Justice Scalia replies to this criticism in his majority opinion explaining that he is not in fact using the legislative history as evidence of Congress' intent. Rather, Scalia explains it was used to show the "extrastatutory influence" congressional committees exert over agencies.

Scalia and Breyer also suggest a different role for the courts regarding judicial review of agency actions under the arbitrary and capricious standard. Breyer notes that had the FCC used notice-and-comment rulemaking, the courts would have required more detailed explanations as to why the agency changed course. Breyer explains that regardless of the fact the agency changed a rule through an adjudicatory decision (instead of notice-and-comment rulemaking), the court in review should reach the same conclusion, that is, more explanation was required. Scalia takes issue with this point by arguing it is not necessary to incorporate all of the APA's notice-and-comment procedural requirements into review of agency adjudicatory decisions under the arbitrary and capricious standard. In other words, Scalia seems to require a different standard for judicial review of agency rules promulgated using notice-and-comment procedures versus agency rules issued through adjudication, whereas Breyer does not.

In summary, Breyer's opinion gives considerable weight to the agency's procedural process, the reasoning methods employed, as well as potential consequences (i.e., effects on local broadcasting) as reasons why the agency change of policy was arbitrary, capricious, and abusive. Breyer also made no use of legislative history to reach that conclusion. In contrast, Scalia's deference to the agency was in large part derived from his textual analysis of the statute and stare decisis of past precedent. Interestingly, Scalia does place weight on the legislative history as evidence for the majority's opinion. It is for the reader to decide whether or not Scalia's use of legislative history was in support of identifying Congress' intent as Stevens alleges, but regardless, it was nevertheless used in support for the majority's reasoning that the agency was justified in changing policy to some extent.

Talk America Inc.

The next case *Talk America Inc.,* involves the FCC's interpretation and application of the Telecommunications Act of 1996, whereby the agency issued a remand order that was interpreted by Michigan Bell Telephone Co. (i.e., AT&T Inc., hereafter AT&T) to allow charging competitive local exchange carriers (LECs) for "entrance facilities" (e.g., wires and cables). The LECs complained to the Michigan Public Service Commission of the new charges and the Commission ruled in their favor. AT&T filed suit in District Court and the Commission's decision was overturned. Interestingly, the District Court relied on an interpretation of the FCC's remand order that differed from FCC's own interpretation put forth in an amicus brief, as evidence the new charges were permissible. The Commission and several competitive LECs, including petitioner Talk America Inc. appealed to the Court of Appeals for the 6th Circuit. The FCC filed an amicus curiae brief to the Court of Appeals explaining the agency's position was to not allow incumbent LECs such as AT&T to charge the higher price for existing facilities and that the District Court was wrong to interpret FCC's remand order as changing the incumbent LECs' interconnection obligations, including the obligation to lease entrance facilities for interconnection. Nevertheless, the Court of Appeals disagreed with the agency's brief and reversed the decision once again in favor of AT&T Inc. The Supreme Court granted certiorari and a unanimous Court reversed the decision yet again.

Justice Thomas wrote the unanimous opinion for the Court and Scalia wrote a separate concurring opinion that revisits the role of judicial review of agency actions, specifically discussing the extent to which courts should defer to agency interpretations of ambiguous regulations promulgated by agencies. First, to the opinion of the Court, Thomas explains that neither the statute nor regulations address whether incumbent LEC must provide access to entrance facilities at cost-based rates or allow the higher rates sought by AT&T. Thomas holds that in the absence of any unambiguous statute or regulation, the Court should assess the FCC's interpretation of its regulation, and does so by using the amicus brief filed to the Court of Appeals. Thomas cites the Court's holding in *Auer v. Robbins* 519 U.S. 452 (1997) that stated courts should defer to the agency's interpretation of a regulation unless the interpretation is, "plainly erroneous or inconsistent with the regulation[s]" or "reason to suspect that the interpretation does not reflect the agency's fair and considered judgment on the matter in question" (461-462). An interesting point raised by AT&T was that the agency's remand order was creating a de facto new regulation through the "guise of interpretation." Recall, under the APA, general notice of proposed rule- making is required with only a few exceptions, including the issuance of interpretative rules. However, Thomas explains that the regulation in question regarding "technically feasible method of obtaining interconnection" is not exhaustive as the regulatory language stipulates the methods "...include, but are not limited to," thus the regulation is interpretive. Furthermore, the Court holds the FCC's interpretation of its regulations is "neither plainly erroneous nor inconsistent with the regulatory text" (2263).

Scalia explains in his concurring opinion that he would join the opinion of the Court without having to resort to *Auer* deference which held that courts defer to an agency's interpretation of its own regulations. Scalia explains that although he has relied on this method of deference in the past he has, "...become increasingly doubtful of its validity" (2266). Scalia's concurring opinion heeds a warning against courts over-empowering agencies. This comes somewhat as a surprise given Scalia's repeated and adamant calling for the courts to return to applying *Chevron* deference to agency interpretations of statutes. To this point, Scalia explains that although the *Auer* precedent seems a "natural corollary" and an "*a fortiori* application" of *Chevron*—where courts defer to an agency's interpretation of an ambiguous statute the agency is charged with implementing—there is a significant difference. Scalia next describes why this is the case by offering a discussion on the separation of powers and the risk of arbitrary government.

Scalia makes a distinction between agency rules that carry the force of law and laws passed by the Congress in terms of power and control. Scalia contends that it is to no benefit (in regards to power) for the Congress to issue vague statutes as agencies will necessarily fill in the statutory gaps as they see fit, thus affording a shift of power to some degree from the Congress to the executive branch. Scalia continues by saying the only option available to Congress to fix or correct the course of action taken by agencies that displeases the Congress is to refine and update the authorizing statutes to remove any such ambiguity that enables an agency's gap filling powers, so to speak.

Scalia makes clear he still supports the application of *Chevron* deference, given the legislative and enforcement actions are separated as *Chevron* deference only applies to the agency's attempts to implement a statute passed by Congress (not the agency). However, Scalia contends that in the instance an agency passes a rule (also carrying the force of law), if the courts simply defer to the agency's interpretation of the rule it distorts the separation of powers by assigning legislative and executive powers to administrative agencies. In other words, *Auer* deference allows the agencies to legislate (through rulemaking) and interpret their own rules for courts to then adhere. Scalia buttresses the point of possible dangers emanating from such deference by quoting Montesquieu, who wrote,

> When the legislative and executive powers are united in the same person, or in the same body of magistrates, there can be no liberty; because apprehensions may arise, lest the same monarch or senate should enact tyrannical laws, to execute them in a tyrannical manner.

Looking towards the future, Scalia notes that by continuing to apply *Auer* deference they are encouraging agencies to continue promulgating vague rules that offer the widest possible interpretation for the agencies to embody in practice and adjudication. Scalia explains the consequence as described regarding this mode of deference, "frustrates the notice and predictability purposes of rulemaking, and promotes arbitrary government" (2266). Scalia closes his concurring opinion by recognizing there are advantages to the standard of *Auer* deference as it makes it easier for reviewing courts to apply the law and also enables consistency across the Circuit Courts, thus "promoting certainty and predictability to the administrative process", but notes he is open to the idea of reconsidering *Auer* in future cases challenging such deference. Scalia's warning of *Auer* deference is taken up again in *Perez v.*

Mortgage Bankers Association and *Decker v. Northwest Environmental Defense Center* discussed further in chapter 3.

City of Arlington

The final FCC case reviewed here is *City of Arlington,* which came about after FCC issued a declaratory ruling to determine the length of time local zoning authorities must act on siting requests submitted by wireless telecommunications companies. Wireless telecommunications networks require towers and antennas and the proposed sites for those towers and antennas must be approved by local zoning authorities. According to 47 U.S.C. §332(c)(7)(B)(ii), state or local governments are required to act on wireless telecommunications networks' siting applications "within a reasonable period of time after the request is duly filed". A complicating aspect of the law that resulted in a split decision were two other features of the statute. Namely, a savings clause that stipulates nothing in the Act, except those limitations provided in §332(c)(7)(B), "shall limit or affect the authority of a State or local government" over siting decisions. Similarly, §332(c)(7)(B)(v) authorizes a person who believes a state or local government's wireless-siting decision to be inconsistent with any of the limitations in §332(c)(7)(B) to "commence an action in any court of competent jurisdiction."

After FCC determined that local authorities were not acting swiftly enough to meet the demand of wireless telecommunications networks, the agency clarified that a "reasonable period of time" is 90 days to process a collocation application (i.e., an application to place a new antenna on an existing tower) and 150 days to process all other applications. The cities of Arlington and San Antonio Texas petitioned for review of the FCC declaratory ruling in the 5th Circuit claiming that the FCC lacked statutory authority to interpret ambiguous provisions of this section of the statute because the saving clause and judicial review provision indicate the Congress never intended the FCC to have authority to interpret the limitations §332(c)(7)(B). The Court of Appeals applied *Chevron* deference and determined that FCC possessed the necessary statutory authority to define the time limitations and that the timeframes were a reasonable construction of the authorizing statute. The Supreme Court granted certiorari to decide whether a court should apply *Chevron* to an agency's determination of its own "jurisdiction".

Scalia writes the 6-3 majority opinion for the Court and explains that there simply is no "jurisdictional" question for courts to consider when it comes to judicial review of administrative discretion and the application of *Chevron*. Scalia holds that there is no distinction between "jurisdictional" and "nonjurisdictional" interpretation and that it is merely a mirage. For Scalia, the real question for the courts is simply whether the agency has gone beyond a reasonable interpretation of the statute. By answering that question, the supposed jurisdictional question of whether or not an agency has exceeded the scope of its authority (i.e., jurisdiction) will have been answered. To show this, Scalia offers a hypothetical statute that reads: 1) No common carrier shall impose an unreasonable condition upon access to its facilities, and, 2) The Agency may prescribe rules and regulations necessary in the public interest to effectuate Section 1 of the Act. To make his point, Scalia then continues the hypothetical by imagining the agency proceeds to pass the following regulations using their authority under section 2:

I. The term "common carrier" in Section 1 includes Internet Service Providers.
II. The term "unreasonable condition" in Section 1 includes unreasonably high prices.
III. A monthly fee greater than $25 is an unreasonable condition on access to Internet service."

Scalia uses this hypothetical to show that the real question for the court is whether the statute gives the agency authority to regulate Internet Service Providers and cap prices. For Scalia, the underlying question of whether the agency can do so does not change using either section 1 or 2 of the hypothetical statute. Rather, the real matter is "whether the statutory text forecloses the agency's assertion of authority, or not."

Scalia heeds a warning that to give this phantom "jurisidictional" question standing would invite judges to substitute their policy preferences to that of the agency. Moreover, the likely effect would be that savvy challengers of agency action would routinely play the "jurisdictional" angle which could put the longstanding judicial doctrine of *Chevron* deference in jeopardy. Scalia also uses this case as a way to distinguish the holding in *Mead*—an opinion whereby he wrote the lone dissent—to clarify that the majority opinion in *Mead* only, "denied *Chevron* deference to action, by an agency with rulemaking authority, that was not rulemaking." Scalia quips that the dissent is unable to produce a "...single case in which a general conferral of rulemaking or adjudicative authority has been held insufficient to support *Chevron* deference for an exercise of that authority within the agency's substantive field." Scalia criticizes the dissenting Justices by saying that their reasoning would result in the courts reverting back to the "totality of the circumstances test" whereby the court would have to search for congressional intent behind every provision of the statute, which would further invite judges to substitute their own preferences and decide for themselves the legislative intent of the statute.

Scalia's attempt to distinguish *Mead* was not missed by Breyer and prompted a separate, yet concurring opinion. Breyer reiterates the value of *Mead* by explaining that a judge, "will have to decide independently whether Congress delegated authority to the agency to provide interpretations of, or to enact rules pursuant to, the statue at issue—interpretations or rules that carry with them the force of law." Breyer leaves the door open to judicial review of agency action by noting that if Congress has not spoken clearly it *could* be a sign that Congress intends the courts to pay close attention to the agency's interpretation. Breyer thinks the Court is to decide independently whether an agency was intended by Congress to provide interpretations to statutes that carry the force of law—and should not be merely assumed. Breyer offers a few things for Judges to consider, such as the agency expertise, importance of the question facing the agency, statutory scheme, legislative history, and subject matter of the relevant provision as it relates to the agency's ordinary statutory duties and expertise. However, Breyer is not really trying to proscribe interpretive rules for Judges, but seems to make the point that each case is unique and judgment will vary as the situation dictates. For example, Breyer notes that, "...our cases make clear that other, sometimes context-specific, factors will on occasion prove relevant".

Ultimately Breyer sided with the majority because he found the petitioners' arguments regarding the judicial review provision and exception clause of the statute to be consistent with a statutory scheme that gives States, localities, the FCC, and reviewing courts each a role to play in the location of wireless service facilities. For Breyer, neither of these provisions is enough to override FCC's plenary authority to interpret the Act under review.

Chief Justice Roberts wrote the dissent for the Court and was joined by Kennedy and Alito. The dissent largely focuses on the separation of powers and the fear that the majority's opinion is further advancing the growth of the administrative state beyond what the founders could have ever imagined, and beyond what the Constitution can allow. For Roberts, "a court should not defer to an agency until the court decides, on its own, that the agency is entitled to deference." Said another way, Roberts writes, "an agency cannot exercise interpretive authority until it has it", and the court should not defer to the agency in answering this question. Interestingly, Roberts cites Breyer's book *Making Our Democracy Work,* specifically a passage that reads, "the president may not have the time or willingness to review [agency] decisions" (110). Roberts uses this passage to further illustrate the point that the judiciary check on administrative action is needed now more than ever given the size of the administrative state and the president's inability to effectively manage such an enormous enterprise. Roberts does not render an opinion on the petitioners' claim that the judicial review provision and exception clause prohibits FCC's interpretation, but instead notes he would have remanding the case back to the 5th Circuit to perform the inquiry in the first instance given in his view the Court should not have permitted *Chevron* deference regarding FCC's jurisdiction. Scalia's opinion acknowledges that Robert's fear of the increasing size and power of the administrative state might be warranted, but that Robert's proposed solution of throwing out the stabilizing effects of *Chevron* deference to allow thirteen Courts of Appeals to apply a totality of the circumstance test in determining jurisdiction would result in chaos.

---

[9]The rule of lenity is the legal tenet that holds ambiguous criminal statutes should be interpreted to favor the defendant and not the government.

[10]During the notice-and-comment period, the agency received more public comments (over 700,000) than it had under any previous time for any subject.

---

[11]In *State Farm*, a unanimous Court decided the National Highway Traffic Safety Administration (NHTSA) did not provide an adequate basis and explanation for rescinding the passive restraint requirement.

CHAPTER 4

Environmental Agency Actions

> ...texts are often silent about permissible reasons for the exercise of agency discretion.
> —Justice Scalia, *Massachusetts v. EPA*

CASE REVIEWS

This chapter begins the review of administrative discretion through the lens of environmental laws implemented through the Department of Interior (DOI), US Army Corps of Engineers (Corps), Environmental Protection Agency (EPA) and its sub-agencies including Fish and Wildlife Services (FWS) Bureau of Land Management (BLM) and National Marine Fisheries Service (NMFS). The six cases reviewed in this chapter involve acts of administrative discretion byway of agency action/inaction, interpretive rules, notice-and-comment rulemaking, and agency interpretation of authorizing statutes.

The first case *Babbitt v. Sweet Home Chapter of Communities for a Great Oregon* 515 U.S. 687 (1995) (hereafter *Babbitt*) involves the Secretary of the Interior's rule clarifying the Endangered Species Act (ESA) and changing the scope of the agency's regulatory purview. This case showcases how legislative history can be used to support or defend administrative discretion. Two cases under review, *Norton v. Southern Utah Wilderness Alliance* 542 U.S. 55 (2004) (hereafter *Norton*) and *Massachusetts v. EPA* 549 U.S. 497 (2007) (hereafter *Massachusetts*) discuss the extent to which agencies have the discretion to *not* act or *not* regulate. These opinions stem from Scalia's unanimous opinion in *Norton*, offering a tutorial about the APA and agency discretion towards inaction, and his dissenting opinion in *Massachusetts* giving reasons why the agency's inaction was permissible. A subsequent companion case *Utility Air Regulatory Group* v. *Environmental Protection Agency (10-1073)* (hereafter *Utility Air Regulatory Group)*, offers both a majority opinion penned by Scalia and contrasting dissent authored by Breyer regarding the EPA's attempt to actuate the Court's ruling in *Massachusetts* which turns on the extent to which an agency can essentially operationalize a statute. In *National Association of Homebuilders v. Defenders of Wildlife* 551 U.S. 644 (2007) (hereafter *National Association of Homebuilders*) Breyer joins the dissent challenging the Court's description of discretionary and non-discretionary agency actions. Breyer writes separately to make clear that agencies are required to take heed of the entire regulatory landscape, including the jurisdiction and responsibilities of other federal agencies. Finally, Scalia and Breyer write separate concurring opinions for the last case reviewed in this chapter, *Coeur Alaska, Inc. v. Southeast Alaska Conservation Council* 557 U.S. 261 (2009) (hereafter *Coeur Alaska, Inc.*), both making the case that the complexity of issues facing the EPA's and Corps's permitting decisions require courts give considerable deference to agency expertise. It is noteworthy to mention that Breyer and Scalia voted together in only 2 of the 6 cases. Also, although Scalia and Breyer both sided with the agency 4 times, this is a bit misleading as Breyer's decision to rule against the EPA in *National Association of Homebuilders* in effect, empowered the regulatory scope and influence of the ESA. Similarly, Breyer's decision not to defer to the EPA in *Massachusetts* was in regards to EPA's decision to not regulate. In other words, this dissent was also calling for the agency to take on additional regulatory power, which Breyer further supports in his dissent in *Utility Air Regulatory Group* where he argues against Scalia and supports EPA to regulate greenhouse gases to curb climate change.

Babbitt

The first environmental case under review involves the DOI and the Director of the FWS, and whether a rule issued by the Secretary of Interior falls outside the purview of the ESA. In *Babbitt,* small landowners and logging companies challenged a regulation claiming the rule improperly broadened the scope of the ESA beyond the intent of the statute. Specifically, the authorizing statute (ESA), states that it is illegal for any person to "take" endangered or threatened species, and defines "take" to mean to "harass, harm, pursue, hunt, shoot, wound, kill, trap, capture, or collect, or to attempt to engage in any such conduct." The Secretary's new rule in question defines "harm" under the statute to include "significant habitat modification or degradation where it actually kills or injures wildlife by significantly impairing essential behavioral patterns, including breeding, feeding, or sheltering." The District Court held that the regulation defining "harm" issued by the Secretary was reasonable and within the confines of the statute. The Court of Appeals affirmed the District Court, but after granting a petition for rehearing, the Court of Appeals reversed.

Stevens wrote the 6-3 majority opinion (joined by Breyer) reversing the Court of Appeals and giving deference to the Secretary's new rule. Stevens uses 3 primary arguments in support of the reasonableness of DOI's new rule, including the (1) text and structure of the Act, (2) legislative history, (3) and the importance of a subsequent amendment. To the first point, Stevens explains that the word "harm" as reasonably understood to include "injury" would fit within the new language specifying injury as a consequence of habitat modification. Stevens notes that the statutory definition of harm does not require "direct" harm (as Respondents and Scalia argue), but also includes indirect harm because to hold otherwise would cause the term "harm" to have no specific meaning in comparison to the other nine words in the Act describing the term "take."

The majority's second argument is that Congress passed the ESA to serve a broad purpose and the Secretary's actions to extend protections for endangered species meets that purpose. Stevens explains that the Court has understood that broad purpose in the past and cites *TVA v. Hill*, 437 U. S. 153 (1978) where the Court in regards to the ESA, said, "The plain intent of Congress in enacting this statute, was to halt and reverse the trend toward species extinction, whatever the cost. This is reflected not only in the stated policies of the Act, but in literally every section of the statute." The majority recognizes that the Respondents "advance strong arguments" marshaling the position that the statute as written does not consider acts causing minimal and unforeseeable harm as violating the "harm" definition of the statute.

However, for Stevens this is not an important factor to consider because the Court was asked to determine if the regulation was impermissible "on its face." In other words, the majority opinion holds the rule is reasonable given the Court is forced to determine the legality of the rule for all possible scenarios, and not any particular action.

Although Breyer did not offer his own separate opinion in this case, it is important to note the majority opinion (joined by Breyer) relies on legislative history as a substantial part of the Court's reasoning to uphold the regulation. Stevens cites both House and Senate Committee reports that accompanied the bills which eventually became the ESA to show that Congress intended the statutory term "take" to be understood broadly and capture direct and indirect actions. Stevens makes note that two similar endangered species bills were introduced to the Senate, whereby a floor amendment added "harm" to the definition, noting that this and accompanying amendments would "help to achieve the purposes of the bill." Stevens' third argument hinges on the fact that Congress passed a subsequent amendment to the ESA authorizing the Secretary to issue permits for takings that would otherwise prohibit, "if such taking is incidental to, and not the purpose of, the carrying out of an otherwise lawful activity." For Stevens, this language makes clear that Congress understood the regulation to "prohibit indirect as well as deliberate" (700).

In summary, Stevens explains that the broad purpose of the statute in combination with the level of administrative expertise necessary to uphold the statute demands the judiciary defer to the agency. To further support this position, Stevens cites the holding in *Chevron* as well as Breyer's 1986 article "Judicial Review of Questions of Law and Policy." Stevens' decision to cite Breyer's article in this instance was perplexing to some extent given this very same article was cited by O'Connor in the *Brown* case discussed in chapter 4. If you recall from *Brown*, O'Connor cited Breyer's article in support of the majority's decision which decided to judicially intervene and *not* defer to the agency.

Scalia's writes a particularly scathing dissent arguing that the majority's opinion "imposes unfairness to the point of financial ruin—not just upon the rich, but upon the simplest farmer who finds his land conscripted to national zoological use" (714). Scalia begins by taking issue with the regulatory language used with respect to the statute. For

Scalia, the Secretary's regulation defining "harm" is not at all reasonable with what Congress scripted in the authorizing legislation. Thus, for Scalia, *Chevron* deference does not apply and that should be the end of the matter. To show *Chevron* does not apply and the regulation is "unreasonable", Scalia challenges the majority's approach to derive meaning from the statutory text and applies a much narrower reading of the statutory term "take." For Scalia, the term "take" (as applied to animals) means nothing more than to "reduce those animals, by killing or capturing, to human control" (717). To support this narrower view Scalia cites two dictionaries published in 1933 and 1949, a Supreme Court case from 1896, as well as a more recent treaty (1973) and federal legislation (1988), all of which use the term "take" on similarly narrow grounds.

Scalia explains that the majority opinion is wrong to apply a broad meaning for the regulatory definition of "harm"—especially when a more narrow definition is permissible—while at the same time giving the authorizing statutory term "take" a narrow meaning. Scalia elucidates more on the methods one should go about deciphering a term that may possibly have separate meanings by making an example for the case at hand. According to Scalia,

> if the terms contained in the definitional section are susceptible of two readings, one of which comports with the standard meaning of "take" as used in application to wildlife, and one of which does not, an agency regulation that adopts the latter reading is necessarily unreasonable, for it reads the defined term "take"—the only operative term—out of the statute altogether. (718)

Furthermore, Scalia contends that it makes more sense to take the narrow view of "harm" as affirmative and intentional acts as opposed to the majority's reading calling for indirect acts, given the other terms (i.e., harass, pursue, hunt, shoot, wound, kill, trap, capture, or collect) used to define "take" also suggest intention. Scalia cites a previous case, whereby Scalia and the Court held when, "several items in a list share an attribute counsels in favor of interpreting the other items as possessing that attribute as well." Interestingly, Scalia does not give this method much weight in the case.

Instead, Scalia offers another factor for agencies to consider regarding how an agency should properly define statutory terms. For Scalia, agency definitions of statutory terms must be applicable to the entire statute. Scalia contends that the Secretary's definition of "take" does not make sense when used in other parts of the statute and offers a few examples whereby the statutory term "take" embodies the narrow and more ordinary meaning throughout the Act. For example, the Act reads, "Congress provided for the forfeiture of "[a]ll guns, traps, nets, and other equipment . . . used to aid the taking, possessing, selling, [etc.]" of protected animals. Scalia quips that to apply the majority's definition of "take" one would expect the statute to include examples such as "plows, bulldozers, and backhoes" (723). In another example, the Act exempts "the taking of any endangered species" by Alaskan Indians and Eskimos "if such taking is primarily for subsistence purposes;" and provides that "[n]on-edible byproducts of species taken pursuant to this section may be sold . . . when made into authentic native articles of handicrafts and clothing" (723). Scalia suggests these examples of the term "take" gives support that the regulatory definition does not comport with the authorizing legislation and is thus impermissible.

Scalia offers another point for judges (and agencies) concerning statutory interpretation by citing *Ratzlaf v. United States*, 510 U. S. 135, 140–141 (1994), which held "statutes should be read so far as possible to give independent effect to all their provisions." Scalia points out that another part of the statute includes contradictory language requiring all federal agencies, "…insure that any action authorized, funded, or carried out by such agency not likely to jeopardize the continued existence of any endangered species or threatened species or *result in the destruction or adverse modification of habitat…*" (emphasis added). Here Scalia is making the point that the agency's definition is hollowing out a separate provision within the statute that is specifically designed to give effect to modification of habitat. Therefore, for Scalia, the Secretary's regulation is invalid as it hollows out meaning for a provision within the actual statute.

Scalia dismisses the majority opinions calling for the EPA to serve a broad purpose and argues it cannot be the case that agency's are able to do most anything to further the purpose of a statute. Scalia describes this purposive method as, "the slogan of the enthusiast, not the analytical tool of the arbiter" (726). However, one would be remiss not to mention that this aspect of the majority opinion clearly falls within Breyer's stated approach calling for a purposive outlook towards statutory interpretation. Continuing the discussion on legislative intent, Scalia takes up the corollary argument of legislative history. Scalia offers a disclaimer that he does not rely on legislative history, suggesting it is not at all a reliable or a legitimate tool of interpretation, but continues on by countering that the legislative history that does exist for this statute does not support the majority opinion. The primary legislative evidence offered by Scalia are quotes from both the House Floor Manager and the Senate Floor Manager that give evidence that Congress does in fact rely on a separate part of the regulation to solve habitat destruction, thus the broadened definition of "harm" as used by the majority opinion contradicts the intention of a separate part of the Act. However, Scalia does concede the majority's point that the Senate Committee Report and the House Conference Committee Report contemplates enabling the Secretary to permit "environmental regulation." To this point, Scalia has no counterargument other than reverting back to his larger theory of jurisprudence that disregards the value of legislative history altogether. Scalia reiterates this position by explaining that that legislative history cannot be used to, "…contradict, rather than clarify what is in its totality an unambiguous statutory text" (730).

Norton

The next case is an interesting look at administrative discretion from the vantage point of agency "inaction" instead of action. In *Norton,* the Court determined whether an agency can use their judgment and discretion to not act, and under what circumstances the courts can compel agency action. Southern Utah Wilderness Alliance and other organizations (hereafter SUWA) filed a lawsuit in the US District Court for Utah against the Bureau of Land Management (BLM), its Director, and the Secretary, alleging that:

- BLM violated its non-impairment obligation under the APA by allowing degradation in certain Wilderness Study Areas (WSA);

- BLM failed to implement provisions in its land use plans relating to off-road vehicle use (ORV);
- BLM failed to take a "hard look" at whether—pursuant to the National Environmental Policy Act of 1969 (NEPA)—it should undertake supplemental environmental analyses for areas in which ORV use had increased.

Under the Federal Land Policy and Management Act of 1976, (FLPMA) the BLM is responsible for keeping an ongoing inventory of federal lands and incorporating a land use planning process that projects present and future use. Prior to the FLPMA, the Wilderness Act of 1964 provides that designated wilderness areas (with some exceptions), shall have no commercial enterprise and no permanent road, no motorized vehicles, and no manmade structures. Although only Congress is allowed to officially designate land as wilderness areas, the BLM does identify "wilderness study areas" (WSA), for large tracts of land (at least 5,000 acres) that include wilderness characteristics as determined by BLM's land inventory. The BLM is required under FLPMA to, "continue to manage such lands…in a manner so as not to impair the suitability of such areas for preservation as wilderness." In addition to the WSAs, the BLM uses "resource management plans"—which are land use plans adopted after notice-and-comment rulemaking—to design and guide future management actions.

The BLM designated approximately 2 million acres in Utah as a WSA and submitted the plan to Congress. SUWA's chief complaint focuses on the permitted use of off-road vehicles for the land designated as WSA, given the known negative effects of off-road vehicles such as soil disruption, compaction, harassment of animals, and annoyance of wilderness lovers. Scalia sums up the problem nicely when he states, "BLM faces a classic land use dilemma of sharply inconsistent uses, in a context of scarce resources and congressional silence with respect to wilderness designation" (2377).

SUWA based their suit on the APA's section 706(1) which permits the courts to "compel agency action unlawfully withheld or unreasonably delayed." The District Court dismissed all three claims and the Tenth Circuit reversed, holding that the agency actions under question were mandatory and non-discretionary duties. Scalia wrote the opinion for a unanimous Court explaining that judicial review of agency inaction in this instance was not appropriate. The opinion provides a tutorial for judges and administrators regarding the limits of judicial review of agency inaction.

First, Scalia explains there is a difference between an agency's "failure to act," and "denial." An example of failure to act is an agency's failure to issue a rule or make a decision by a statutory deadline, whereas a denial is an agency action, for example saying no to a request. Scalia makes clear that an agency's failure to act is discretionary by nature. Scalia follows that under the APA, the courts should only review "failure to act" cases for instances whereby the agency failed to take a discrete agency action that the agency is required to take. In such a case, the courts can compel agency action, but still cannot specify what the action must entail. Scalia explains that the APA's limitations on court review of agency action helps to, "protect agencies from undue judicial interference with their lawful discretion, and to avoid judicial entanglement in abstract policy disagreements which courts lack both expertise and information to resolve" (2381). For Scalia, if courts were to interpret the APA otherwise would, "...inject the judge into day-to-day agency management" (2381). SUWA argues that the BLM's land use plan "obligated BLM to conduct an intensive ORV monitoring program" and the agency's authorizing statute requires BLM manage "in accordance with" land use plans, as well as the regulatory requirement that authorizations and actions "conform to" those plans.

Scalia makes a distinction in this case by explaining a statement in an agency's plans indicating future actions are distinct from required agency actions. According to the Court, a statement in a plan that "will take this, that, or the other action" in the future is not a binding commitment that courts can intervene and compel agencies to implement. Scalia points to the regulations stating land use plans are, "designed to guide and control future management actions and the development of subsequent, more detailed and limited scope plans for resources and uses" as evidence the land use plans in question are future oriented. Scalia notes that to require agencies to implement initiatives from planning documents as opposed to decisions would result in courts prioritizing agency actions. Moreover, some agency plans are targeted far into the future and can go beyond the agency's knowledge of future budget allocations. Thus, courts calling for implementation can disrupt the agency's ability to plan as necessary and prioritize actions, especially actions that are constrained by budgets. Finally, the Court dismisses SUWA's argument that NEPA requires the agency to give a "hard look" at whether to undertake supplemental environmental analyses for areas in which ORV use had increased because the land use plan is a "proposed action." Scalia distinguishes a "major federal action" (requiring hard look review pursuant to NEPA) in this case as the actual "approval process," whereas the land use plan is only a planning document discussing future actions.

Massachusetts

In *Massachusetts* the Court examining once again the extent to which agencies are required to act and under what circumstances agency inaction is permissible. This case stems from a rulemaking petition issued by 19 private organizations requesting the EPA begin regulating greenhouse gas emissions from new motor vehicles under the Clean Air Act (CAA). In response to the petition, the EPA asked for comments regarding any "scientific, technical, legal, economic or other aspect of these issues" and received over 50,000 comments within a 5 month period. Afterwards, the EPA issued an order stating the agency lacked statutory authority to regulate greenhouse gas emissions, and further noted that even if the agency had the authority it would not do so because it would be unwise to do so at the current time. Petitioners, joined by States and local governments, challenged the EPA's order in the US Court of Appeals for the District of Columbia Circuit, whereby the Circuit Court determined that the "EPA Administrator properly exercised his discretion under §202(a)(1) in denying the petition for rule making."

Justice Stevens (joined by Breyer) wrote the 6-3 majority opinion reversing the Circuit Court and remanding the case back to the EPA for further proceedings. The Petitioners asked the Court to determine whether EPA has the statutory authority to regulate greenhouse gas emissions from new motor vehicles; and if so, whether its stated reasons for refusing to do so are consistent with the statute. However, in addition to Petitioner's question for the Court, a substantial legal hurdle was first addressed concerning whether the Petitioner's had standing to sue. In fact, it is this legal point that takes up Chief Justice Robert's entire dissenting opinion (joined by Scalia). The topic of standing is not especially relevant for the purposes of this research project focusing on administrative actions, thus the lengthy arguments both for and against the legal issues regarding standing are not discussed here. Suffice it to say, the majority opinion held that sovereign States are not normal litigants for the purposes of invoking federal jurisdictions and the elements necessary to acquire legal standing such as injury, remedy, etc., were considered adequate by the majority.

The more salient issue for the purposes of administrative law was whether the EPA rightfully interpreted their role with respect to the CAA, and if so, whether the agency's reasoning for inaction was arbitrary, capricious, or an abuse of discretion. To follow the textual argument, noted below is the CAA statute in question,

> The [EPA] Administrator shall by regulation prescribe (and from time to time revise) in accordance with the provisions of this section, standards applicable to the emission of any *air pollutant* from any class or classes of new motor vehicles or new motor vehicle engines, which in his *judgment* cause, or contribute to, air pollution which may reasonably be anticipated to endanger public health or welfare . . . (emphasis added)

The CAA further defines "air pollutant" as "*any* air pollution agent or combination of such agents, including *any* physical, chemical, biological, radioactive . . . substance or matter which is emitted into or otherwise enters the ambient air" (emphasis added). For Stevens, the word "any" as part of the definition for air pollutant makes the statute unambiguously clear on the point that carbon dioxide is an air pollutant subject to regulation.

Interestingly, the EPA explains that the Supreme Court decision in *Brown* (discussed in the previous chapter) was part of the agency's reasoning as to why the agency should not get involved. According to EPA's understanding of the precedent set in that case, the EPA does not have the power to initiate such a sweeping regulation on limiting greenhouse gases, as this would most likely have even greater economic and political repercussion than regulating tobacco, which the Court struck down.[12] Furthermore, the EPA drew a similar comparison with FDA, explaining that climate change legislation has its own unique political history and Congress has never specifically called for the regulation of greenhouse gases to curb climate change. With that in mind, the EPA reasoned the statutory term "air pollution" is better defined as not including greenhouse gases within the meaning of the CAA. In addition, EPA noted that if greenhouse gases were defined as air pollutants under the statute, the primary method to limit such emissions would require fuel efficiency regulations. Yet, the EPA explained that Congress already passed a statute requiring the Department of Transportation (DOT) to enforce fuel standards, thus any regulatory act on EPA's part in that regard may contravene DOT's clearly mandated responsibilities.

Stevens explains for the Court that the holding in *Brown* was different because in the event the agency were to regulate tobacco, the likely result would be an outright ban on tobacco—whereas in this case the EPA would simply regulate and not ban emissions. Furthermore, the EPA does not have a long history whereby the agency made clear it does not regulate emissions, unlike the FDA which long held it did not have jurisdiction over tobacco. In regards to the potential regulatory overlap between EPA and DOT, Stevens explains that the agency mandates are distinct and set apart. For example, the EPA is charged with protecting public health and welfare, whereas DOT is charged with promoting energy efficiency. For Stevens, this separation of mandated authority does not permit EPA to "shirk" from its primary responsibilities.

Next, Stevens addresses the legal question of whether the agency inaction was arbitrary, capricious, or abusive discretion. Stevens explains that the agency's decision to not regulate is based on factors outside the authorizing statute. For example, the EPA explains the political nature of the issue and that any regulatory measures taken could inhibit the President's ability to negotiate with other countries to reduce emissions. This argument is not convincing to Stevens, as he argues the statute is unambiguous and thus the, "...EPA can avoid taking further action only if it determines that greenhouse gases do not contribute to climate change or if it provides some reasonable explanation as to why it cannot or will not exercise its discretion to determine whether they do" (533). In other words, Stevens makes clear that agencies must reason their rulemaking decisions on the authorizing statute, and not extraneous factors that are not germane to the overriding legislation. Finally, Stevens responds to the agency's claim that the science is still developing and regulatory measures taken would be premature, by explaining that an agency cannot simply note a few scientific uncertainties and decide to not then regulate as required by statute. Instead, if the agency reasonably assess the science is profoundly in question, the agency must explain this position and not simply avoid regulatory measures.

As stated previously, Chief Justice Roberts' dissenting opinion (joined by Scalia) is entirely based on the issue of standing and is therefore not addressed here. However, Scalia wrote a separate dissenting opinion that goes beyond standing and addresses the Court's opinion in full, discussed next.

Scalia begins by taking up the argument over what factors of consideration are relevant for administrative agencies. Scalia explains that it is right for agencies to consider "outside" factors as those listed by EPA, including the decision to not engage in an "inefficient, piecemeal approach", given the President's vision calling for a "comprehensive approach" that considers "near-term voluntary actions and incentives along with programs aimed at reducing scientific uncertainties and encouraging technological development" (551). In short, Scalia derides the majority's opinion limiting agency discretion to statutory matters as having, "no basis in law" and unreasonable in practice given it is necessary and proper for agencies to consider other executive branch programs including foreign policy.

Scalia opines that although he disapproves of the majority's newfound boundaries for administrative discretion; nevertheless, in this case it is an irrelevant factor. Scalia explains, "the statute says nothing at all about the reasons for which the Administrator may defer making a judgment the permissible reasons for deciding not to grapple with the issue at the present time" (552). Scalia continues by saying, "...the statutory text is silent, as texts are often silent about permissible reasons for the exercise of agency discretion" (552).

Next, Scalia begins the textual analysis of the EPA's interpretation of the statutory term "air pollutant." Scalia makes the case for his contrasting definition (which aligns with the agency's definition) by-way of a legal grammar lesson of sorts. Scalia first concedes the majority's definition of air pollutant is also reasonable; however, Scalia's larger point on the matter is that the agency interpretation is clearly within the bounds of reason, and thus the Court is wrong to replace their definition of "air pollutant" with that of the agency. Scalia explains that so long as the agency interpretation of an ambiguous statute is reasonable, the Courts should defer to the agency interpretation as *Chevron* dictates.

Scalia closes his argument by accusing the majority as simply enforcing its own policy preference on the issue of climate change and subverting the Executive Branch's attempt to implement the law. For Scalia this is a "straightforward administrative law case," and the Court "has no business substituting its own desired outcome for the reasoned judgment of the responsible agency" (560).

In summary, this was an interesting case whereby the majority's decision *not* to defer to the agency may actually create more regulatory power and influence for the agency moving forward. It is noteworthy that in this case the majority opinion also put forth an interesting precedent that attempts to constrain agency decision-making by eliminating external factors—not cabined within the statute itself—as unreasonable factors for agency consideration. In this respect, the decision actually constrains administrative discretion to some extent. It is also interesting that despite the Court's change of position regarding the amount of administrative discretion afforded under *Brown*, both Breyer and Scalia were consistent. In both cases Breyer deferred to the agency's position and Scalia did not.

Utility Air Regulatory Group

EPA's regulatory power is explored further in the next case, *Utility Air Regulatory Group*. This case is a directly related companion case decided in 2014 whereby the EPA tries to implement the Court's opinion in *Massachusetts* by regulating greenhouse gases due to its affect on climate change. Scalia writes the majority opinion and Breyer writes a separate opinion that concurs and dissents in part.

After the *Massachusetts* case was decided the EPA promulgated rules to regulate greenhouse gas emission standards for new motor vehicles. By classifying greenhouse gases as an air pollutant subject to regulation, the EPA determined that other provisions of the CAA were also triggered, as different permitting requirements apply to stationary sources with regards to regulated air pollutants. The EPA recognized that the regulatory impact was monumental as it would require the EPA to begin regulating and permitting many smaller industrial sources (e.g., large office and residential buildings, hotels, large retail establishments) as greenhouse gas emissions are much larger in magnitude than conventional pollutants. EPA recognized that including greenhouses as an air pollutant would create an "unprecedented expansion of EPA authority that would have a profound effect on virtually every sector of the economy and touch every household in the land". Therefore, EPA issued a notice of proposed rulemaking to allow the public and industry to share their views on how to respond to the Court's decision in *Massachusetts.* The EPA attempted to strike a balance with the statutory language that specifies the amount of pollution that triggers the permitting requirements, by "tailoring" the statute byway of an agency interpretation that allowed much higher levels of greenhouse gas emissions before necessitating permitting so that the EPA could continue with regulating the large source entities that were fewer in number and accounted for the majority of pollution. Numerous parties including several states filed petitions for review in the D.C. circuit challenging EPA's actions and the court dismissed some of the claims for lack of jurisdiction including EPA's tailoring rule, but upheld that the statute required EPA to conclude that a source's greenhouse gas emissions necessitate a Prevention of Significant Deterioration (PSD) and Title V permit. The Supreme Court granted six petitions for certiorari but only reviewed one question, "whether EPA permissibly determined that its regulation of greenhouse gas emissions from new motor vehicles triggered permitting requirements under the CAA for stationary sources that emit greenhouse gases." Scalia wrote the majority opinion for a split 5-4 decision, and Breyer wrote the dissent.

Scalia begins by distinguishing the precedent set in the *Massachusetts* decision—a decision that he did not join as discussed above—by arguing the Court merely held that the Act-wide definition of "air pollutant" includes greenhouse gases because it is all encompassing and it "embraces all airborne compounds of whatever stripe." However, according to Scalia, the term "air pollutant" in the Act's operating provisions carries a much narrower meaning and claims that the EPA has also given the term a narrower and "context appropriate meaning". In support of this position, Scalia provides examples whereby the EPA has interpreted provisions of the CAA that discuss "any air pollutant" to apply to narrower meanings such as, "..for which the area is designated nonattainment", and limited to "visibility-impairing air pollutants" instead of every substance falling within the larger Act-wide definition. Scalia uses these examples to make clear that the Court did not invalidate the agency's longstanding constructions of the statute in *Massachusetts*, but simply held that the EPA must "ground its reasons for action or inaction in the statute". Scalia leans on the Court's earlier decision in *Brown* to show the importance of considering words of a statute within context and also within the larger statutory scheme, beyond the particular statute under review—a point that seems in some ways contradictory to a literalist method of jurisprudence, especially given the CAA is reviewed here in isolation and *Brown* turned largely on the fact no *other* laws supported FDA.

Next, Scalia begins his review of EPA's decision to use a tailoring rule to adjust the threshold for permitting decisions to essentially make the statute reasonable and actionable. Scalia reviews EPA's rule using *Chevron*, and determines that EPA's decision was not reasonable and therefore inappropriate. Namely, Scalia points out that "an agency has no power to tailor legislation to bureaucratic policy goals by rewriting unambiguous statutory terms." For Scalia, the statute says in no uncertain terms that permits are required for sources with the potential to emit more than 100 or 250 tons per year of a relevant pollutant. EPA's attempt to tailor the threshold to 100,000 tons per year for greenhouse gases specifically as a way to limit the number of establishments that would be affected by the statute was considered unreasonable. Scalia cites *National Association of Homebuilders* (discussed more below) to show that agencies must, "give effect to the unambiguously expressed intent of Congress." In Scalia's view, the agency cannot replace numbers with others of its own choosing without violating their statutory authority.

Scalia adds to his literalist and separation of powers argument by also noting that if the EPA's tailoring rule were upheld, then the EPA would be awarded "newfound authority to regulate millions of small sources—including retail stores, offices, apartment buildings, shopping centers, schools, and churches". Scalia uses *Brown* again to support that when an agency claims to discover in a long-extant statute new and significant powers to regulate, the Court approaches this with skepticism and assumes that Congress would make clear such regulatory measures carrying economic and political significance. Before moving on to Breyer's dissent, it is worth noting that both Justices agreed that the EPA did reasonably interpret the Act to require sources to comply with "best available control technology' emission standards for greenhouse gases—a position that Alito wrote separately to criticize.

Breyer's dissent supports EPA's decision to regulate greenhouse gases and makes clear that the agency's use of technical expertise and administrative experience in creating the threshold rule for greenhouse gas emissions is the type of decision that Congress typically leaves to agencies. Breyer agrees with Scalia that a generic reference to "any air pollutant" need not include every substance falling with the Act-wide definition, but disagrees with the Court's holding that there is an atextual greenhouse gas exception to the phrase "any air pollutant". Breyer claims a more sensible approach that better fits with the legislative history—as evidenced in a senate report—as well as the common sense purpose of the statute would be to read an implicit exception for small-scale greenhouse gas emissions into the phrase "any source". For Breyer, finding flexibility in "any source" allows the statute to work in practice. Breyer takes a stab at Scalia's literalist approach to the use of "any air pollutant" by noting that a more realistic view of the language in the statute would be to assume that Congress was not merely trying to arrange "words on paper" but attempting to achieve "real-world purpose".

Breyer adds that the EPA recognized that Congress did not intend the EPA to regulate all sources prior to greenhouse gas regulations due to the threshold rules already in place. For Breyer, the agency was attempting to meet the spirit of the statute by creating a similar threshold that makes sense for regulating greenhouse gases—similar to the pre-existing statutory limitations regarding permitting for other air pollutants. Scalia addresses the crux of Breyer's dissent in a footnote by stating that, "we are aware of no principle of administrative law that would allow an agency to rewrite such a clear statutory term, and we shudder to contemplate the effect that such a principle would have on democratic governance."

Another note on this case is Alito's separate opinion that accuses the majority opinion of selectively applying a literalist interpretation with regards to the term "pollutant", where in one part of the statute it is considered narrowly, and in another part broadly. According to Alito, "the Court's literalism is selective, and it results in a strange and disjointed regulatory scheme."

National Association of Homebuilders

The next case reviewed here is *National Association of Homebuilders*. In this case the relevant question before the Court was how the EPA's responsibilities under the Clean Water Act's (CWA) requirements (and as the dissenting opinion explains, possibly all agency actions) are influenced by the Endangered Species Act (ESA). Specifically, the ESA requires that, "agencies insure that any action authorized, funded, or carried out by such agency…is not likely to jeopardize the continued existence of any endangered species or threatened species." Similarly, the EPA has its own set of regulations under the CWA regarding how the agency must go about transferring permitting powers to states that apply and meet nine specified criteria.

In this case Arizona applied to EPA for the rights to implement the National Pollution Discharge Elimination System (NPDES) which is designed to prevent harmful discharges into the Nation's waters. The EPA determined that Arizona met all of the 9 criteria under the CWA to appropriately oversee the permitting process, but prior to transferring authority to the state the EPA first consulted with the Fish and Wildlife Service (FWS) as required under the ESA. The FWS determined that transferring the permitting responsibilities from the EPA to Arizona was permissible and did not adversely affect any endangered species. However, FWS raised a concern regarding the ESA's jurisdiction, noting that once the authority is transferred to the state, subsequent permits issued by the state will not require that the state first consult with FWS prior to issuing permits. FWS asked the EPA to consider the possible cumulative effects of the state's permitting decisions in the future as part of EPA's factors to consider prior to granting permitting rights to the state.

The EPA determined that its authorizing statute (CWA) did not allow for this extra criterion as part of the decision making process. The agencies consulted again to reach agreement on the issue as part of a memorandum of understanding and the FWS changed its position and issued a biological opinion concluding that the "requested transfer would not cause jeopardy to listed species and the loss of...conservation benefits . . .is not an indirect effect of the authorization action." Respondents filed a petition in the United States Court of Appeals for the Ninth Circuit which held the FWS revised opinion was not permissible and EPA's reliance on it was "arbitrary and capricious," thus the Circuit Court denied the transfer of permitting authority to the state.

Justice Alito writing for a 5-4 split Court, authored the majority opinion (joined by Scalia) which reversed and remanded the 9th Circuit's decision. Alito explained the EPA's actions were not arbitrary and capricious merely because EPA's holding was in part due to FWS revised opinion. In other words, FWS was free to change its opinion prior to the final rule and moreover the EPA followed notice-and-comment procedures for 45 days allowing interested parties to provide input regarding the State program. Alito further held that the CWA's statutory language is mandatory through use of the term "shall" and the list of 9 criteria is exclusive. In other words, the agency does not have discretion to deny a transfer application for any reason outside of the 9 criteria attached to the CWA. This distinction of non-discretionary decision was crucial for the majority opinion in distinguishing possible agency actions as arbitrary and capricious. In this case, so long as the EPA makes the transfer/permitting decision on the 9 criteria, there is simply no opportunity to act arbitrarily or capriciously as no discretion is afforded through the Act.

Alito points out that the agencies charged with implementing the ESA (i.e., FSW and the NMFS) issued a regulation using notice-and-comment rulemaking procedures explaining that the ESA requirements under review here "applies to all actions in which there is discretionary federal involvement or control." Alito emphasizes the term discretionary in the above definition and reasons that given the EPA's decision in this case is non-discretionary, the ESA's requirement is not relevant to the EPA when determining whether to transfer permitting rights to a state. The majority opinion gives a very narrow definition regarding administrative discretion. Specifically, the majority opinion says the term discretion "presumes that an agency can exercise judgment in connection with a particular action," and supplements this description with a dictionary definition stating discretion has the "power or right to decide or act according to one's own judgment."

Justice Stevens authored the dissent (joined by Breyer) and explained the majority's definition of discretion is problematic, if for no other reason the very action of determining whether the State meets the CWA requires discretion on the part of the EPA, thus contradicting the majority's proposition that the agency has no discretion at all. According to Stevens, "the EPA's approval of a State application to administer an NPDES program entails significant indeed, abounding discretion..." (694). Moreover, the dissent argues that the majority opinion misreads the ESA by emphasizing the term "discretion," and should instead focus on the definitional-statutory language suggesting there is no distinction between mandatory and discretionary action as "action" is defined by the ESA in relevant part:

> Action means all activities or programs of any kind authorized, funded, or carried out, in whole or in part, by Federal agencies in the United States or upon the high seas. Examples include, but are not limited to actions intended to conserve listed species or their habitat and the promulgation of regulations...

For Stevens, the majority's decision to use the term discretionary as a way to constrain action creates a contradiction in the EPA regulation itself. The dissent adds that prior Court precedent, legislative, and regulatory history does not support the majority's opinion. In short, the dissent argues the Court has long held that Congress has intended for the ESA to have significant importance regarding agency actions and should be considered as part of all agency actions which might affect the habitats of endangered species. Stevens' dissent declares that EPA's decision was in fact arbitrary and capricious under the APA and should be remanded back to the agency for further review.

Breyer's brief and separate dissenting opinion takes root where Justice Stevens ends discussing the extent to which all agencies should or should not consult with FSW and NMFS regarding agency actions potentially impacting ESA. Breyer makes clear he is not willing to decide at this juncture whether all agencies, including unrelated agencies, would need to consult with FSW and NMFS as seemingly stipulated by ESA. Breyer gives a disclaimer that he is not going as far in his decision to determine for example, whether a discretionary determination by the IRS to prosecute or settle a particular tax liability is required to conform to the ESA. However, Breyer then goes on to offer a few hypothetical examples of why the majority opinion's contention that the structure of the CWA precludes application of the ESA to the EPA's discretionary action is wrong.

Breyer states that, "grants of discretionary authority always come with some implicit limits attached" (698). Breyer offers a few hypothetical examples to illustrate this point, including a description of the FDA which has statutory authority to enforce an exclusive list of criteria in determining whether a new drug will get agency approval. Breyer explains that in the event the FDA found potential for the manufacture and/or marketing of a new drug to impact the preservation or destruction of an endangered species—since the passage of the ESA—those factors should be considered by FDA despite the FDA's authorizing statute not including such information as part of the agency's criteria to review new drugs. Breyer also notes that *TVA v. Hill* 437 U.S. 153 (1978) is the binding Court precedent and cites the case to show how since the passage of ESA, the regulatory landscape, "indicates beyond doubt that Congress intended endangered species to be afforded the highest of priorities" and moreover, the ESA "demonstrated a conscious decision by Congress to give endangered species priority over the primary missions of federal agencies" (699).

Breyer's dissenting opinion is concise, but taken together with the fact he joined the dissent, it is clear that Breyer is searching for a functional and harmonizing approach between the two statutes that maintains the purpose of the ESA without requiring the abjection of administrative discretion through a definitional focus on the CWA. Although Breyer ultimately rules against the EPA in this case by not deferring to the agency's interpretation of the statute, he does so to preserve other agencies' scope and power in the future. Breyer's decision shows his willingness to consider the consequences of judicial decisions in the long term and signals his disproval for the likely effects the majority opinion will bring about, namely constraining the scope and impact of the ESA and the agencies charged with carrying out the statute's provisions.

Coeur Alaska, Inc.

A similar case involving the EPA and CWA was decided in *Coeur Alaska, Inc.* Breyer and Scalia both wrote separate concurring opinions for this case agreeing with the judgment of the majority opinion. However, Breyer writes separately to clarify what the dissent regards as a regulatory loophole and Scalia revisits the application of *Chevron* deference to agencies.

Similar to *National Association of Homebuilders*, in *Coeur Alaska Inc.*, the Court was once again faced with how to harmonize two seemingly contradictory regulations across two different agencies. Specifically, how does the EPA's permitting responsibility regarding the discharge of pollution intersect with the US Army Corps of Engineers (Corps) permitting responsibility for discharging fill material? The petitioner in this case (Coeur Alaska) had plans to open a gold mine and begin using a "froth flotation" technique to churn the mine's crushed rock in large tanks of frothing water to expel gold materials. As part of this plan, petitioner received a permit from the Corps to discharge "slurry" (i.e., mixture of crushed rock and left over water at the bottom of the tank) into a lake. According to the EPA and the Corps, the slurry was defined as "fill material" given it will rise the bottom of the lakebed approximately 50 feet, thus the permit was issued by the Corps in agreement with the EPA. Petitioner then obtained a separate permit from the EPA for the purposes of discharging processed water from the lake where the slurry is collected, into a downstream creek.

The EPA has the authority to regulate the amount of pollutants that certain categories of new sources may discharge into navigable waters. The majority opinion reiterates that pursuant to this authority, the EPA issued a new source standard restricting discharges from new froth-flotation gold mines. The standard explicitly states that mines allow, "No discharge of process wastewater." Respondents brought suit claiming the Corps permit was invalid and was in fact the wrong agency to issue the permit. Respondents argued that Section 402 of the Clean Water Act granting the EPA authority to issue a permit for the discharge of any pollutant required that EPA issue the permit, and not the Corps. In addition, respondents argued that regardless of who issues the permit, the permit is illegal under the new source standard that prohibits the discharge of process wastewater from mines.

The US District Court for the State of Alaska granted summary judgment in favor of Coeur Alaska Inc. The Court of Appeals for the Ninth Circuit reversed and gave weight to the EPA's new source performance standard prohibiting discharges from froth flotation mills. Thus, the Circuit Court invalidated the permit from the Corps, and also explaining that an EPA permit would not suffice either given the prohibitive regulation. Justice Kennedy (joined by Scalia and Breyer) authored the majority opinion for a 6-3 Court reversing the Circuit Court and holding the Corps' permit as valid.

Kennedy's majority opinion relies on the agency procedural safeguards to some extent noting that by continuing to allow the Corps permitting authority for discharging fill material from a mine (despite the CWA seemingly contradictory terminology regarding new source prohibitions under the EPA authority) the EPA still has veto authority over the Corps' permitting decision. In this case, the Corps followed the standards set-forth by the EPA outlining how the Corps should go about determining the fill material permit and the EPA did not overrule the Corps' decision. In contrast to the petitioners' contention that the EPA new source rules carves an exception regarding the Corps's permitting jurisdiction, Kennedy determines that the shared agency model is workable. The majority opinion shows sensitivity to industry by explaining to rule otherwise would create a burden, forcing dischargers to ask whether a fill material is "subject to EPA's many hundreds of performance standards…" (276).

After solving the jurisdictional question, the majority opinion next turned to the question of whether the permit was in fact lawful given the EPA's rule targeting discharge material from mines. Kennedy explains that the statute is ambiguous, requiring the agency interpretations as the next step of inquiry. However, the agency interpretations are also ambiguous, so the next step of the inquiry is to see how the agencies have practiced under existing ambiguous guidelines. In other words, how are the ambiguous regulations understood in practice?

Kennedy points to a memorandum of understanding as a way of answering how the agencies understand and interpret their regulatory scheme and responsibilities. In doing so, Kennedy notes that the memo does not warrant *Chevron* deference to the agency's interpretation of their authorizing statute given the memo is not the same as formal procedures (e.g., such as notice-and-comment proceedings), but is owed some level of deference given it is instructive regarding the regulatory scheme—a point Scalia revisits in his concurring opinion. According to the memo,

> As a result [of the fact that the discharge is regulated under §404], the regulatory regime applicable to discharges under section 402, including effluent limitations guidelines and standards, such as those applicable to gold ore mining . . . do not apply to the placement of tailings into the proposed impoundment [of Lower Slate Lake]. See 40 CFR §122.3(b).

Kennedy explains five major points about the memo and why it is salient to the legal question at hand. For Kennedy, the memo:

1. preserves a role for the EPA's performance standard,
2. acknowledges that this is not an instance in which the discharger attempts to evade the requirements of the EPA's performance standard,
3. preserves the Corps' authority to determine whether a discharge is in the public interest,
4. does not allow toxic pollutants to enter the navigable waters,
5. sensible and rational construction that reconciles §§306, 402, and 404, and the regulations implementing them (287)

In summary, the majority decides to defer to the EPA's conclusion that the performance standard does not apply and the permit was correctly authorized by the Corps, thus reversing the 9th Circuit.

Breyer's separate but concurring opinion is aimed at addressing the administrative demands and procedural processes in place to address the difficult undertaking of classification and regulation as evidenced by this case. Breyer takes heed of the dissent's warning which claims that, "whole categories of regulated industries" might "gain immunity from a variety of pollution-control standards" if a permit applicant uses language suggesting a pollutant is actually a fill material to gain the regulatory system (293). Breyer's willingness to vote with the majority—given the dissents poignant warning of a regulatory loophole—seems to be primarily based on the procedural safeguards the agencies possess to overcome this concern. Namely, the EPA can still veto the Corps permitting decisions.

Breyer agrees that the EPA and Corps interpretation of what constitutes "fill material" is reasonable, thus legal. However, Breyer goes to considerable length explaining the varieties of discharges that fall under the performance standards and notes the new source performance and effluent limitation regulations are over 800 pages. Breyer also points out the regulations are additionally numerous with respect to the various chemicals, minerals, and other substances that are produced at the point source already under regulation. Breyer's pragmatic jurisprudence comes into focus as he illustrates the complexities facing administrators and emphasizes their need to apply judgment as circumstances dictate. Breyer explains that the ruling today may still require some level of judgment on part of the Corps and EPA moving forward amidst the numerous complexities at issue in these types of cases. Although Breyer goes along with the majority opinion, it is clear that he is somewhat concerned the ruling may be inappropriately used in the future as some sort of bright line test that can be used for similar cases. Breyer concludes his opinion by conceding he is not sure if the compromise EPA agreed to regarding this particular case produced the best environmental result, but the compromise does "amount to the kind of detailed decision that the statutes delegate authority to the EPA, not the courts, to make (subject to the bounds of reasonableness)" (294).

Scalia's very short opinion concurring in part and in judgment takes issue with the majority's description regarding the amount of deference owed to the memorandum in an effort to determine the agency's position. Namely, Scalia explains that the majority's opinion purporting to side-step *Chevron* deference and instead evoke *Auer* deference (i.e., *Auer v. Robbins* 519 U. S. 452 (1997) which established the principal that judicial deference is owed to agency interpretations of agency ambiguous regulations)) was incorrect. According to Scalia, the Court actually applied *Chevron* deference given the Court relied on a memo to primarily understand the ambiguous statutes, and less so the agency regulations.

Scalia goes on to lament the effects resultant from the *Mead* case (discussed in chapter 1), which according to Scalia has caused a continued state of confusion regarding how and when *Chevron* deference is applicable. Scalia cites an article and 6 court cases as evidence that the courts are confused and do not know how to apply the holding in *Mead.* For this case, Scalia explains that the Court's deference to the EPA and the Corps is "eminently reasonable" and the "vast body of complex laws committed to the charge of executive agencies" requires some assurance the courts will "accept reasonable and authoritative agency interpretation of ambiguous provisions" (296). In closing, Scalia quips that he would overturn *Mead*, but "failing that, I am pleased to join an opinion that effectively ignores it" (296).

Ginsburg's dissent follows the 9th Circuits reasoning and holds that the EPA's strict standard concerning new source standard leaves no room for the permit issuance. More interesting for this project is Ginsburg's critique of Breyer's concurring opinion whereby she explains the "safeguards Breyer identifies are hardly reassuring" (303). For Ginsburg it is "optimistic to expect that EPA or the courts will act vigorously to prevent evasion of performance standards" (303). Ginsburg also points out that EPA's veto power cannot substitute for the contradictory regulations regarding the new source standard, and also notes the EPA has only used this veto authority a dozen times over 36 years during which more than one million permit applications have taken place. Ginsburg says that, "reliance on ad hoc vetoes, moreover, undermines Congress' aim to install uniform water-pollution regulation".(303).

---

[12]For the purposes of this project, it is worth pointing out that the EPA's reference to the holding of *Brown* as a primary reason to not regulate gives some credence to the influence of Court decisions on administrative discretion. Albeit, in this case the EPA's attempt to apply Court precedent was unsuccessful given the Court distinguished the prior case and called for agency regulation.

CHAPTER 5

Department of Labor Agency Actions

> If statutes are to serve the human purposes that called them into being, courts will have to continue to pay particular attention in appropriate cases to the experience-based views of expert agencies.
> —Justice Breyer, *Christensen v. Harris County*

CASE REVIEWS

This chapter takes a look at Breyer's and Scalia's approach towards administrative discretion as embodied through the Department of Labor (DOL). Specifically, this section includes 4 cases covering administrative discretion byway of notice-and-comment rulemaking, substantive rules, agency interpretation of authorizing statutes, and agency interpretation of agency rules.

The first case *Christensen v. Harris County* 529 U.S. 576 (2000) (hereafter *Harris County*) reviews the Fair Labor Standard Act (FLSA) and highlights both Judges' contrasting views on judicial deference and what circumstances call for courts to defer to agency interpretations of ambiguous statutes. The following 3 cases *Long Island Care at Home LTD., v. Coke* 551 U.S. (2007) (hereafter *Coke*) and *Christopher v. SmithKline Beecham Corp*. 567 U.S. (2012) (hereafter *Christopher*) and *Perez, Secretary of Labor et al., v. Mortgage Bankers Association* No. 13—1041 (2014) (hereafter *Perez*) serve as excellent companion cases for review. In the *Coke* case, Breyer writes for a unanimous Court and gives a tutorial on when and how agencies are supposed to fill statutory gaps through agency rulemaking. In this case the Court makes a distinction between agency proposed rules and final rules, explaining the extent to which courts respect of the administrative actions should differ to allow for administrative flexibility and adaptability. The follow-up case *Christopher,* finds the Justices at odds, as Scalia deviates from the unanimous opinion in *Coke*, and instead votes to overturn the Secretary of Labor's interpretation of the authorizing statute. Breyer's dissent takes note of this change of course and reminds the Court that the *Coke* opinion already determined the authorizing statute in question was ambiguous, requiring the DOL to effectuate the legislation. Finally, in the most recent *Perez* case, a unanimous Court determines that judicial deference to an agency's interpretation of their own regulation has limits with respect to the authorizing legislation. Justice Scalia and Thomas write separate concurring opinions that go further to demonstrate judicial deference to agency regulations creates constitutional problems. Scalia and Breyer vote together in 2 of the 4 cases.

Harris County

The first of the FLSA cases under review, *Harris County,* includes both a dissenting opinion from Breyer and a concurring opinion from Scalia. In this case, Texas Deputy Sheriffs challenged the County's decision requiring employees to schedule time off to use their compensatory time earned. This rule prevented the County from having to make cash payments to employees in lieu of compensatory time earned. The County enforced this rule in light of a perceived-possible budget shortfall which would make paying the employees' accrued compensatory time very difficult. Interestingly, the County sent a letter to the DOL's Wage and Hour Division, asking if it was permissible for the County Sheriff to schedule non-exempt employees to take compensatory time. The Acting Administrator of the Division replied to the County explaining that the employer's actions are permissible so long as there is a pre-existing agreement between the employee and employer to that effect. In response to the letter, the County initiated the new rule despite not having a pre-existing agreement with their employees.

The deputy sheriffs argued (similar to the DOL's opinion letter) that FLSA does not permit an employer to compel an employee to use compensatory time without an agreement between the employee and employer to do so in advance. The District Court held the County violated the FLSA and the U.S. Court of Appeals for the 5th Circuit reversed holding that the FLSA and DOL regulations do not prohibit employers from applying this requirement upon employees.

Justice Thomas authored the 6-3 majority opinion (joined by Scalia) affirming the Court of Appeals. The majority opinion relied on the fact that the FLSA statute does not expressly prohibit the employer from requiring employees to use their compensatory time, a point the respondent's concede. Whereas the petitioner's claim the statute implicitly prohibits the County's practice, the majority opinion determines the statutory language is only a safeguard to ensure that employees receive compensation for over time in a reasonable amount of time and nothing more. Justice Stevens' dissenting opinion (joined by Breyer) argued that the key issue is not the fact the statute does not include a prohibition, but rather the general employee/employer rule requiring an "agreement" as encompassing the manner in which the compensatory time may be used from the onset. The issue taken under discussion by both Breyer's and Scalia's separate opinions is the question of whether or not the courts should defer to the agency's opinion letter provided to Harris County explaining that a pre-existing agreement is necessary to meet the intention of the FLSA. The majority opinion disregarded the opinion letter and the dissenting opinion deferred to the agency letter's interpretation of the law. Justice Scalia filed a separate opinion concurring in part and concurring in the judgment for the purposes of clarifying his differing method of applying *Chevron* (i.e., judicial deference to administrative interpretation of statutes). Breyer's dissenting opinion is aimed only at addressing the concurring opinion authored by Scalia.

Staying with the majority opinion for a moment, Scalia argues in his concurring opinion that the majority's claim that *Skidmore* deference is relevant as a secondary consideration—after determining *Chevron* does not apply—is incorrect. For Scalia, the *Skidmore* decision is an "anachronism" and has been replaced with the Court's more recent *Chevron* decision which holds that the courts cannot "substitute its own construction of a statutory provision for a reasonable interpretation made by the administrator of an agency." For the majority opinion, (and Breyer's dissent) if the courts decide that *Chevron* deference is unwarranted, the courts are still correct to defer to agency interpretations of law to the extent that the agency interpretation is persuasive given their technical knowledge and experience, regardless if the agency's action constitute an exercise of delegated lawmaking authority. Breyer summarizes this point succinctly when he writes,

> to the extent there may be circumstances in which *Chevron*-type deference is inapplicable—e. g., where one has doubt that Congress actually intended to delegate interpretive authority to the agency (an "ambiguity" that *Chevron* does not presumptively leave to agency resolution)—I believe that Skidmore nonetheless retains legal vitality. (596-597)

In this case, Scalia does not decide whether or not the DOL's opinion letter is the position of the agency and warrants deference, but he does mention that the Solicitor General's amicus brief co-signed by the Solicitor of Labor agreeing the opinion letter is in fact the agency position on the issue does warrant *Chevron* deference. Scalia goes on to explain—via a footnote addressing Breyer's dissent—that Breyer's position requiring Judges to determine whether Congress actually intended to delegate interpretive authority to the agency is not a factor up for consideration. Instead, Scalia explains that *Chevron's* precedent requires Judges presume that ambiguities are to be resolved (within the bounds of reasonable interpretation) by the administering agency. Scalia claims there are only 3 possible reasons why the courts should not invoke *Chevron* deference:

1. the statute is unambiguous, so there is no room for administrative interpretation;
2. no interpretation has been made by personnel of the agency responsible for administering the statute; or
3. the interpretation made by such personnel was not authoritative, in the sense that it does not represent the official position of the expert agency.

In this case, Justice Scalia agrees that *Chevron* deference is applicable, but the interpretation offered by the agency's opinion letter does not meet the *Chevron* standard which requires the agency interpretation rendered is "reasonable," thus he joins the majority opinion in judgment and does not defer to the agency. For Breyer, the DOL's position is reasonable using either the *Chevron* lens, *Skidmore* lens, or both (597).

Coke

In the case of *Coke*, Breyer authored a unanimous opinion regarding whether or not the Department of Labor's (DOL) regulation adding further definition to the meaning of the Fair Labor Standards Act (FLSA) was permissible. This case took root when a home healthcare attendant sued her employer for over time and minimum wage rights allegedly guaranteed to her under FLSA. According to FLSA, individuals "employed in domestic service employment to provide companionship services for individuals…unable to care for themselves" are exempted from the maximum hours and minimum wage rules. The agency regulation in question labeled "Interpretation" stated the FLSA exemption includes those "companionship" workers "employed by an agency other than the family or household using their services." However, DOL's general regulations define the statutory term "domestic service employment" as "services of a household nature performed by an employee in or about a private home . . . of the person by whom he or she is employed." In other words, the agency regulation expanded the FLSA exemption to those domestic service employees paid by a third party, and does so despite a general regulation definition that seemingly contradicts the broader exemption by narrowing it to only those employees who perform work of the person by whom he or she is employed.

The District Court sided with the government and determined the agency regulation was binding and controlling. The U.S. Court of Appeals for the Second Circuit reversed noting that the regulation was under a section titled "Interpretations" giving weight the rule was merely interpretive, and agency interpretations of law are not entitled to *Chevron* deference. Breyer's unanimous opinion held the agency regulation as binding and valid. The unanimous opinion is essentially a tutorial on how agencies are to interpret and use discretion regarding their mission with respect to the statutes they are charged with implementing. Quoting *Chevron*, Breyer begins by noting that an agency's power to administer a congressionally created program necessarily requires the making of rules to fill any gap left, implicitly or explicitly, by Congress. Moreover, when an agency reasonably fills a gap left by a statute and follows procedural requirements, the agency action is legal (165). For Breyer, this is exactly the scenario facing the DOL as the FLSA explicitly leaves gaps regarding the scope and definition of "domestic service employment" and "companionship services."

After determining the agency is necessarily filling a statutory gap, the next question for this case is how to sort through the seemingly contradictory agency regulation and statutory language. Breyer takes note of the potential consequences of ruling against the agency's regulation by noting that to override the agency in this case would "create serious problems as to the coverage of particular domestic service employees by the statutory exemption or by the FLSA as a whole" (169). Moreover, the primary purpose of the agency regulation is to precisely define the manner in which the exemption applies to third party employers, whereas the contradictory-statutory language's primary focus is to describe the type of work that meets the definition of "domestic service" employee, and not the scope of exemptions. Given the agency regulation is much more specific to the legal question of whether or not a third party is exempted from FLSA, the Court reasoned the more specific agency regulation governs. Finally, the Court explains the agency underwent the rulemaking notice-and-comment procedures thus avoiding the charge that the agency was arbitrarily changing their method of statutory interpretation without signaling the change to the public.

The Respondent's primary argument to the Court was that the regulation was an interpretive rule that merely described the law and was not intended to act as a regulatory measure that changes the statute's scope. Respondent's point out the Court's precedent has been to not afford *Chevron* deference to agency interpretative rules. Respondent also argues the regulation in question is described under the heading "Interpretation", thus demonstrating the regulation is nothing more than an interpretive rule. However, Justice Breyer explains that under the APA, agency-interpretive rules do not require notice-and-comment and yet the agency employed those rules for this regulation suggesting the agency intended this as more than an interpretation, but a legally binding rule promulgated through DOL's rulemaking authority. Breyer also notes that the Court assumes Congress will expect the courts to treat an agency regulation as an effort to fill statutory gaps when the rule affects important individual rights and duties as in this case, and the agency focuses fully and directly upon the issue and uses full notice-and-comment procedures also employed in this instance. Breyer explains the agency's decision to veer from the original agency proposal—which did not exempt some large enterprise third party employers—to later adopting a final rule that exempted all third-party-employed companionship workers from FLSA was a logical outgrowth of the proposed rule and thus legally permissible. Breyer makes the distinction of an agency proposal that shows the rule is under consideration, versus a final rule, which for the Court can reasonably depart from a proposed rule so long as it is reasonable. The majority opinion did not rely on any legislative history and stated the respondent's attempt to do so in support of their position was unavailing.

Christopher

The next case reviewed, *Christopher* is a near identical case questioning whether the FLSA exemptions of minimum wage and maximum hours applied to "outside salesman." However, in this instance Scalia did not defer to the agency and instead joined the majority opinion overturning the agency's interpretations of the authorizing statute.

In this case, two pharmaceutical representatives sued their employer (i.e., SmithKline Beecham Corporation) alleging overtime pay and liquidated damages were owed to them under the FLSA. The pharmaceutical representatives' job duties were primarily focused on delivering information to prescribing doctors in an attempt to garner non-binding agreements from the doctors to prescribe the company's drug. This process is referred to as "detailing." The petitioners' incentive pay was based on the amount of sales or market share the representative's assigned drugs achieved in their particular sales territory, and the representative routinely worked over the 40 hour maximum for regular pay under FLSA. The U.S. District Court for the District of Arizona granted summary judgment to the employer ruling that pharmaceutical representatives were exempt as "outside salesman" under FLSA. The petitioners filed a motion (which the District Court rejected) to amend the judgment, arguing that the court failed to grant deference to the DOL's interpretation of the pertinent regulations that was announced in an amicus brief filed by the DOL regarding a similar case under review in the Second Circuit. In that brief and subsequent amicus briefs the agency explained that that pharmaceutical detailers are not exempt under FLSA. However, the Court of Appeals for the Ninth Circuit affirmed the District Court and agreed that deference to the agency interpretation was not owed.

Justice Alito wrote the 5-4 majority opinion (joined by Scalia) for the split Court and held that the agency's position on the exemption status of pharmaceutical detailers is not entitled to judicial deference. Justice Alito explains that although the agency's position has remained unchanged regarding pharmaceutical detailers as non-exempt employees, the reasoning the agency has used to support that position should be questioned by a Court if the outcome is "plainly erroneous or inconsistent with the regulation," or if the agency's interpretation "does not reflect the agency's fair and considered judgment on the matter in question." For Alito, it is the latter consideration that significantly impacts the case given the agency has only first announced its view that pharmaceutical detailers do not qualify as outside salesmen byway of filing amicus briefs. In other words, the agency's interpretive rule was not made available for public comment as there was no notice-and-comment period. Alito explains it is unfair for the agency to place an enormous financial burden on the pharmaceutical industry without first making the regulatory definition clear. Alito also makes note of the fact that the industry itself has long been treating pharmaceutical detailers as exempt employees and DOL has never once initiated any enforcement actions against pharmaceutical companies or suggested the industry was acting against the law.

After Alito determines the Court owes no deference to the agency's own vague regulations—a precedent normally dictated under *Auer*—he next turns to the statutory language to determine if the agency's regulations are consistent with the authorizing statute. In summary, the majority makes the case that various statutory terms such as, "consignment for sale," "any," "other disposition" and "includes" (instead of "means"), and many other terms support their position that the most reasonable interpretation of the authorizing statute requires that the term pharmaceutical salesman fits within the statutory language of "outside salesman," and are thus exempt.

Justice Breyer writing for the dissent focuses on the statutory language and comes to the opposite conclusion that pharmaceutical detailers are non-exempt and are not "outside salesman." Breyer begins by restating the authorizing statute which states, "any employee employed . . . in the capacity of outside salesman as such terms are defined and delimited from time to time by regulations of the Secretary" are exempt. Breyer cites *Coke* discussed previously as an example of the Court having already agreed the FLSA was ambiguous on this topic and requires the agency to fill the statutory gaps. Thus, for Breyer the agency is right to determine the meaning of the statute and Breyer first turns to the regulations to get a foothold on what the statute should mean in practice. In doing so, Breyer notes the primary regulatory language in question reads that an employee's "primary duty" must be "making sales within the meaning of section of the Act", and the Act says that the word "sale" or "sell" includes any sale, exchange, contract to sell, consignment for sale, shipment for sale, or other disposition."

Breyer explains that the reader would have to give the words above special meaning to extrapolate that a pharmacy detailer fits within those terms. Namely, this is so for Breyer because although the pharmaceutical detailer may get the prescriber to agree to prescribe a particular drug when that particular prescribing scenario arises, it is still the pharmacist and not the detailer who ultimately sells the drug. Breyer reasons this is partly the case simply because the pharmacist can choose to offer a generic or brand name version at the time of sale. Breyer furthers this claim by pointing out the Department of Health and Human Services estimates showing that 75 percent of prescriptions are filled by generic drugs.

Breyer turns to agency definitions as put forth by the DOL's Wage and Hour Division Report written in 1940 describing the work of "sales promotion men" who "pave the way" for sales by others and are primarily interested in sales by the retailer, not to the retailer. The report declares that these employees, "are admittedly not outside salesmen." For Breyer, these definitions hold true to pharmaceutical detailers given that detailers are primarily intended to provide information and promote the drugs to doctors who can authorize sales, but the detailer does not sell directly to the doctor. Similarly, Breyer cites a Wage and Hour Division Report written in 1949 that defines a company representative as someone who,

> ...visits chain stores, arranges the merchandise on shelves, replenishes stock . . . , consults with the manager as to the requirements of the store, fills out a requisition for the quantity wanted and leaves it with the store manager to be transmitted to the central warehouse of the chain-store company which later ships the quantity requested.

The report goes on to say that this example of a company representative is not an "outside salesman" because he "does not consummate the sale nor direct his efforts toward the consummation of a sale (the store manager often has no authority to buy)." For Breyer, this analogy holds true for pharmaceutical detailers as they promote products and arrange for potential sells in the future, but just as store managers, the doctors do not have authority to buy the drugs. In the case of medicine, the doctor is only authorizing later sales among different parties. Moreover, Breyer notes that it would be against medical practice anyway for doctors to prescribe a drug that does not fit the diagnosis. In other words, the marketing and non-binding commitment of a prescribing doctor cannot trump a doctor's medical decision to prescribe the best suited drug to address the patient's needs.

The most interesting aspect of Breyer's dissent for the purposes of this project is his non response to the procedural questions brought forth by the majority opinion. Breyer's dissent appears to fall neatly within a literalist and definitional argument—that one may expect to come from Scalia or Thomas—concerning terms described in regulations promulgated during the 1940's by the DOL. Breyer does not take issue with the fact that 60 years has passed whereby the agency did not take executive action or address the exemption in regards to pharmaceutical detailers at any time and the industry had long assumed and functioned with the assumption that pharmaceutical detailers are exempt from FLSA. Breyer's deference to the agency's interpretation absent of any notice-and-comment procedures shows a very strong inclination on his part to defer to the agency.

Perez

Finally, the most recent *Perez* case revists the FLSA once again and Sotomayor writing for a unanimous Court holds that notice-and-comment procedures are not required when an agency changes an interpretation of their own regulations. However, Scalia, Thomas, and Alito write separate-concurring opinions which go further to make clear that although they agree with the ruling in this case, in their opinion judicial deference to agency interpretations of their own regulations runs afoul of the Constitution and separation of powers doctrine.

In this case the DOL's Wage and Hour division is once again at center stage along with the FLSA and the role of agency notice-and-comment procedures. In 2004, DOL's Wage and Hour division promulgated a revised regulation that affected the administrative exemption for overtime payments under the FLSA. Following this new regulation, the Respondent, Mortgage Bankers Association (MBA) requested an interpretation of the new regulation as it relates to mortgage-loan officers, and in 2006 the Department provided their new opinion holding that mortgage-loan officers now qualify for the administrative exemption. This 2006 decision was a change in precedent as prior to the 2004 revised regulation the Department had issued letters in 1999 and 2001 stating mortgage-loan officers do not qualify for the exemption. However, in 2010 the Department reversed their decision again by rescinding the 2006 opinion and issuing an Administrator's Interpretation that determined mortgage-loan officers no longer qualify. A key factor for the case was the fact that the Department changed precedent from the 2006 opinion without undergoing notice-and-comment procedures. MBA claimed that the Department's newfound position was arbitrary and capricious under the APA as the interpretation did not comport with the actual 2004 regulation. More central to the case was MBA's claim that the Department's reversal was procedurally invalid given that prior court precedent (*Paralyzed Veterans of America v. D.C. Arena L.P.*) requires agencies to undergo notice-and-comment procedures when an interpretation substantively deviates from prior agency interpretations.

The Court's unanimous opinion was seemingly made easy given the specific statute under review for this case (i.e., APA) has an explicit provision which states unless, "notice or hearing is required by statute," the Act's notice-and-comment requirement "does not apply…to interpretative rules." (553(b)(A). For the majority opinion, this was the end of the matter as the statutory provision so clearly stated cannot override judicial precedent requiring notice-and-comment for substantive changes to agency interpretations of regulations. Sotomayor makes clear that given an agency is not required to use notice-and-comment procedures to render an initial interpretive rule, it follows that an agency is not required to undergo notice-and-comment procedures when it amends or repeals an interpretive rule.

Sotomayor's opinion goes on to explain the role of the Court regarding the APA when she writes, the Court "…trust[s] that Congress weighed the costs and benefits of placing more rigorous procedural restrictions on the issuance of interpretive rules" when developing the APA. It is this portrayal of the APA's construction that led to Scalia, Thomas, and Alito's writing separate concurring opinions.

Scalia's separate concurring opinion attacks the notion that Court's decision vindicates Congress' understanding of the balance of power and procedure within the APA during its enactment. To demonstrate how far the Court has veered from Congress' initial intent he points out that the APA has a clause which states "the reviewing court shall…interpret constitutional and statutory provisions, and determine the meaning or applicability of the terms of an agency action." (§706) Thus, Scalia makes the point that Congress likely intended and assumed courts would review all instances of agency interpretations of both statutes and regulations. Therefore, the APA's exemption of interpretive rules from notice-and-comment procedures were quite modest in terms of agency power as the courts were to determine whether the law/regulations under review means what the agency has interpreted it to mean. Interestingly, Scalia admits that the Courts have a long history of ignoring this aspect of the APA and instead the Court has created judicial doctrine such as *Chevron* deference, which allows agencies to resolve statutory gaps, and *Auer* deference which assumes agencies are to resolve regulatory gaps. It was surprising to see that Scalia, who endorses textualism, and is arguably the Court's loudest proponent and defender of *Chevron* deference, admit that the Court essentially replaced the text of the APA with judge-made doctrines. However, Scalia caveats that at least in the case of *Chevron* the Court has a long history of judicial review of executive action where statutory ambiguities were left to reasonable resolution by the Executive, whereas the *Auer* deference has no such history.

Scalia continues drawing a distinction between the Court's application of *Chevron* and *Auer* deference by noting that there are good reasons to not allow an agency the power to write ambiguous laws and then determine what that ambiguity means. Scalia references a 2013 separate opinion he wrote for *Decker v. Northwest Environmental Defense Center* concurring in part and dissenting in part which details these reasons.[13] Specifically, Scalia makes clear in the case that to allow agencies to be judge of their own regulations creates an imbalance in the separation of powers and encourages agencies to purposely create regulations that are vague so they can then redefine the regulations through interpretations as necessary. For Scalia, if the courts' default position is to defer to the agencies interpretations then the agencies are arguably assuming too much power—something the APA was trying to avoid. Scalia concludes by saying that to remedy this problem, the Court merely needs to discard the concept of *Auer* deference and apply the statute as written. Namely, the courts should allow the agencies to interpret its own regulations with or without notice-and-comment, but re-instill the courts' responsibility of determining—without affording any deference to the agency—whether the agency's interpretation is correct.

---

[13]*Decker v. Northwest Environmental Defense Center* was not included as part of the case analysis because Breyer did not participate in that opinion.

CHAPTER 6

Department of Justice and IRS Agency Actions

> Agencies may play the sorcerer's apprentice but not the sorcerer himself.
> —Justice Scalia, *Alexander v. Sandoval*

CASE REVIEWS

This chapter begins the review of three separate cases; two involving the Department of Justice (DOJ) and one case involving the Internal Revenue Service (IRS). In *United States v. Fior D'Italia, Inc.*, 536 U.S. 238 (2002) (hereafter *Fior D'Italia Inc.*), the Court was faced with determining whether IRS agents' method of levying taxes on a local business were within the limits of the authorizing legislation. In this case there was no specific rule promulgated by the IRS under review, only the actions taken by the IRS agents. Breyer writes the majority opinion ruling the IRS method of taxation is valid, affording considerable discretion on the part of IRS agents, whereas Scalia joins the dissent which argues the discretion afforded to the agency creates an unduly burden on private businesses. The DOJ cases under review include the Court's analysis of agency discretion byway of a substantive and interpretive rule issued by DOJ in *Alexander v. Sandoval* 532 U.S. 275 (2001) (hereafter *Sandoval*) and *Gonzales v. Oregon* 546 U.S.243 (2006) (hereafter *Oregon*) respectively. Breyer and Scalia find themselves at odds again as both Justices disagree in each case whether the promulgated rules go beyond the agency's discretionary power. Scalia writes the majority opinion for *Sandoval* and the dissenting opinion for *Oregon*, and Breyer joins the opposing opinions of the Court in both cases. In summary, Scalia and Breyer did not vote together for any of these cases. However, Scalia's vote agreed with the federal agency position for 1 of 3 cases, while Breyer agreed with the federal agency's position for 2 of 3 cases.

Fior D'Italia Inc.

In *Fior D'Italia Inc.*, a restaurant brought suit challenging the IRS's method of assessing employer FICA tax liability. Specifically, the IRS adopted a method to assess the restaurant for FICA taxes based upon tips the restaurant employees may have received but did not report. By law, employees who receive wages in the form of tips must report the amount of those wages to the employer, who must send copies of those reports to the IRS. In 1991 and 1992 the employees provided the required reports to Fior D'Italia restaurant, and eventually the IRS, and Fior D'Italia paid the FICA taxes based on that reported amount. However, the same report showed that customers had listed tips on their credit card slips for amounts far exceeding the employee reported amounts. The IRS realized the discrepancy and conducted a compliance review. The IRS used an "aggregate estimation" to determine the likely non-reported tip wages by examining the restaurant's credit card receipts for the years in question and used the average of those tips (14.49 % in 1991, and 14.29 % in 1992) as the assumed rate for cash paying customers and then multiplied the average rate for the total receipts, the result of which resulted in additional taxes levied against the restaurant. The question for the Court was whether the agency's actions were out of step with the IRS's authorizing tax statute. More specifically, whether the "aggregate estimation" method was an acceptable practice for assessing tax liability, or whether the law requires the IRS to determine total tip income by estimating each individual employee's tip income separately, then adding individual estimates together to create a total.

The District Court decided the aggregate estimation method did not fall within the IRS's statutory authority and ruled in favor of Fior D'Italia. The Court of Appeals affirmed the District Court and noted that at minimum the IRS needed to adopt its own authorizing regulation as a procedural matter before simply applying a new method of tax assessment. The Supreme Court granted the government's petition for certiorari and Justice Breyer authored the majority opinion that reversed the lower courts in a 6-3 decision. Justice Scalia joined Justice Souter's dissent.

Justice Breyer's begins his opinion by noting that the Court has a long tradition of upholding various IRS tax estimation methods and that the method in question only needs to meet a "reasonable" standard to satisfy the Court. The first legal question at issue is whether or not the statute itself allows for an aggregate method or demands an individual tax liability assessment. The respondent, as well as the dissenting opinion, give weight to a textual argument that shows FICA taxes are attached to individual payments and thus the aggregate estimation method employed is impermissible with respect to the statute. The text provision used to support this position reads, "imposed on every employer" an "excise tax" calculated on the basis of "wages . . . paid by him" as those "wages" are "defined" in the statute. The term wages includes tips, and tips are defined as "received by an employee in the course of his employment" (244).

Breyer's majority opinion explains that this narrow textualist reading focusing on the singular language "makes too much out of too little" (244). Namely, Breyer notes that the language written as singular only appears in the definitional section of the statute, whereas the operational clauses of the statute uses plural language such as "wages" and "individuals." For Breyer, the narrow definitional phrasing couched in the singular does not speak for the whole of the statute and therefore does not prohibit the agency's estimation method.

After Breyer dispels the linguistic argument, the next question is whether or not the method employed meets the reasonable standard. The respondent and dissenting opinion put forth a few arguments to support the claim that the aggregate method is unreasonable. First, the law excludes an employee's tips from the FICA wages base when the tips are less than $20 a month as well as the portion of tips and other wages (including fixed salary) that rise above a certain threshold ($53,400 in 1991 and $55,500 in 1992), therefore the aggregate method can overestimate the amount of tips the employee owes under the right conditions. For example, if a waitress earns $40,000 in salary and reports $20,000 in tips and fails to report $5,000 in tips the restaurant would not owe additional taxes, because the reported income ($56,000) already exceeds the FICA limit. Although Breyer recognizes this scenario as a distinct possibility, Breyer points out that it is also the case that an employee's combined salary and tip amount may not total the FICA ceiling, and thus any tips received and not reported would cause the employer to incur an additional tax liability. For Breyer, the fact that either scenario is possible is reason enough to support that IRS's aggregate estimate method is not unreasonable.

Second, the respondent argues that cash paying customers are known to leave smaller tips and sometimes no tips. Moreover, sometimes customers paying by credit card leave a high tip on the card but then ask for some cash back resulting in a smaller tip amount than what shows on the receipt, and some companies deduct the credit card company fee from the tip leaving a smaller tip for the employee and thus a smaller FICA tax liability for the employer. Nonetheless, Breyer's majority opinion notes that these considerations are not enough to consider the agency's methods unreasonable. For Breyer, the alternative solution of performing individual audits will likely result in the same set of problems as these audits are also based on individual estimates. Breyer also does not sympathize with the restaurant's claim that they do not have the needed information (i.e., tips received but not reported) to challenge an IRS assessment. Breyer explains that a restaurant should be able to determine how many employees were likely to have earned more than the FICA ceiling, how much on average cash-paying customers tip, and whether a credit card deduction is applied to employee tips. In addition, in the event a restaurant challenges an assessment, the restaurant does not have to precisely demonstrate the aggregate estimate method resulted in an unfair FICA tax levy, but rather, must only show that the method most likely produced an inaccurate result to succeed in court. Breyer's position in this case offers the agency considerable discretion, even at the expense of requiring taxpayers undergo extra steps to formulate their tax obligations or challenge taxes levied against them.

The most interesting argument addressed for the purposes of this project was the respondent's allegation that the aggregate method was simply a tool IRS developed to force employers into signing up for the "Tip Reporting Alternative Commitment" program. IRS agreed to develop this special program as a way for the IRS to only levy taxes on reported tips so long as the restaurant puts in place accurate tip reporting measures. The complicating factor is the Internal Revenue

Service Restructuring and Reform Act of 1998, 112 Stat. 755 which specifically prohibits the IRS from "threaten[ing] to audit" a restaurant in order to "coerce" it into entering the special tip-reporting program. Respondent argued that the aggregate estimate method forces restaurant owners into verifying, investigating, monitoring, and enforcing tax compliance on its employees. Thus, according to the respondent, the agency's discretionary actions are not only unreasonable, they are coercive and abusive. Breyer disagrees with the allegation by explaining that the respondent has only shown the aggregate estimation method may lend itself to abusive agency action, but there is no evidence of the agency acting illegally in this case. Breyer calls for significant levels of agency discretion when he rebuts the respondent's claim of agency abuse by saying, "But we cannot find agency action unreasonable in all cases simply because of a general possibility of abuse—a possibility that exists in respect to many discretionary enforcement powers" (251).

Justice Souter's dissenting opinion (joined by Scalia), accepted each of the respondent's claims outlined above. Souter explains the majority's broad reading of the statute in question places an undue burden on employers which is something the Congress never intended. It is noteworthy that this argument relies to some extent on competing statutes and less so on the authorizing statute in question. The dissent emphasizes the text of the statute as requiring the singular approach as the only permissible interpretation, but also argues the statute functions better and faces less contradictions and anomalies when read as plural—contrary to the majority's reasoning. The dissent finds it unfair for the IRS to penalize an employer for the failure of the employee, and takes refuge in the statute's provision which states, employers do not need to keep records "in connection with charged tips" other than "charge receipts, records necessary to comply with section 6053(c), and copies of statements furnished by employees under section 6053(a)" (256).

Souter also points out that despite the majority's assumption that an individual tax assessment method may equally be plagued by errors, for Souter, at least an individual assessment will determine if the employee's salary meets the FICA ceiling rule. This alone would increase the accuracy of the FICA tax levied against the employer. Interestingly, the dissenting Justices also agreed with the respondent's allegation that the IRS was most likely trying to coerce the restaurants into monitoring and enforcing their employees' adherence to tax laws. Souter notes the agency actions are "suspicious" in that regard and that it was also "difficult to imagine that Congress would allow the aggregation practice as a lever on employers…" (262).

Sandoval

The next case under review, *Sandoval* was a case that answered whether an individual had standing to bring suit and enforce disparate-impact regulations promulgated by the Department of Justice under Title VI of the Civil Rights Act of 1964 (Act). Although the primary legal question turns on the question of standing instead of regulatory action or interpretation, the case (especially the dissent) goes to considerable length in describing the scope and relation of authorizing statutes and agency rules and was thus deemed relevant for the purposes of this project. The case arose from the Alabama Department of Public Safety's (Department) decision to only administer state driver's license examinations in English. Important for this case is the fact that the Department received financial grants of assistance from the US Department of Justice (DOJ) and Department of Transportation (DOT), thus the agency is bound by the federal requirements of the Act. Section 601 of the Act ensures no person shall, "on the ground of race, color, or national origin, be excluded from participation in, be denied the benefits of, or be subjected to discrimination under any program or activity." The statute also authorizes federal agencies "to effectuate the provisions of section 601, ". . . by issuing rules, regulations, or orders of general applicability." Under this authority, the DOJ issued a rule forbidding funding recipients to "utilize criteria or methods of administration which have the effect of subjecting individuals to discrimination because of their race, color, or national origin…." Sandoval brought a class action lawsuit to the US District Court for the Middle District of Alabama arguing the Department's English only driver license test violated the DOJ regulation because it discriminates against non-English speakers. The District Court sided with Sandoval and enjoined the policy, requiring the Department to make arrangements for non-English speakers. The Court of Appeals for the Eleventh Circuit affirmed, and the Supreme Court granted certiorari and reversed.

Scalia wrote the 5-4 majority opinion holding the disparate impact agency regulations do not include a private right of action as does section 601 of the authorizing statute. For Scalia, section 601 of the Act permits disparate impact and only prohibits "intentional" discrimination. Thus, the agency regulations that go beyond intention and prohibit disparate impact (i.e., actions that lead to unintentional adverse effects on a protected class) do not afford an individual a right of action to enforce the agency regulations as would be the case for challenging the Act itself. A subtle but important distinction here is the majority is not challenging whether the agency regulation is valid, only what power an individual has to enforce agency actions with respect to the statute. Albeit, based on the tone of the majority's opinion, one may reasonably assume had the agency's rule been directly challenged with respect to the statute, the majority would have likely struck the rule as impermissible as well, or at least very questionable. This observation gains traction in light of Scalia's footnote which challenges the dissent's description of the regulation and statute's shared goal when he writes, "...how strange it is to say that disparate-impact regulations are 'inspired by, at the service of, and inseparably intertwined' with the Act, when the Act permits the very behavior that the regulations forbid" (286 fn6). Unlike the dissent, the majority opinion finds the discussion of the scope of agencies' discretionary-authority under the Act as "beside the point" and the only question is whether the regulation "confers a private right of action to enforce them."

Scalia cites the holding from *N. A. v. First Interstate Bank of Denver, N. A.*, 511 U. S. 164 (1994) stating a "private plaintiff may not bring a suit based on a regulation against a defendant for acts not prohibited by the text of the statute," to make clear the distinction between a rule and statute. For Scalia, the private right to sue the agency in an effort to enforce the regulation in question must derive from the independent force of the agency regulation. Scalia explains that if the statute does not grant such standing, then an agency's failure to comply with the regulation, but not the statute, is not actionable. In other words, a private right to challenge the agency flows from the statute and not the regulation, unless the regulation invoking the statute meets the statutory intent.

Scalia makes clear that the legislative history the dissenting members of the Court rely on in part for their decision is not persuasive, and moreover is not legitimate. Scalia explains the Court has never, "...accorded dispositive weight to context shorn of text. In determining whether statutes create private rights of action, as in interpreting statutes generally, legal context matters only to the extent it clarifies text" (288). According to Scalia, the majority opinion can "...begin (and find that we can end) our search for Congress's intent with the text and structure of Title VI" (288). Scalia makes the distinction that the "rights creating" language is found in the Act reading "no person . . . shall . . . be subjected to discrimination," but the regulation alone cannot require such standing for individuals. Scalia explains, the "language in a regulation may invoke a private right of action that Congress through statutory text created, but it may not create a right that Congress has not" (291). Scalia's position on this regulation/statutory distinction of rights to individuals is succinctly captured with the quote provided at the beginning of this chapter, where he states in this case, "Agencies may play the sorcerer's apprentice but not the sorcerer himself" (291).

The dissenting opinion was written by Justice Stevens and joined by Breyer, Ginsburg, and Souter. Stevens argues the principles of standing regarding agency action under law have been well established and Congress has intended the courts to provide remedy and hear cases under the Act. According to Stevens almost every appellant court has either explicitly or implicitly upheld that a private right of action exists to enforce all of the regulations issued pursuant to Title VI, including the disparate-impact regulations. Stevens cites numerous cases as support of this position, including 12 Circuit cases that explicitly found the private right of action as valid. For Stevens, the case should not have even been reviewed by the Supreme Court, but in so hearing, the Court should have simply deferred to past precedent and decided the case under stare decisis.

The more interesting part of the dissent as related to this project is the administrative tutorial provided about the relationship of agency regulations and authorizing statutes. According to the four dissenting Justices, the majority does not accurately take into account the role of the agency and the Congressional expectation that agencies implement broad statutory language. Stevens begins by describing section 601 of the statutory text under review that states:

> No person in the United States shall, on the ground of race, color, or national origin, be excluded from participation in, be denied the benefits of, or be subjected to discrimination under any program or activity receiving Federal financial assistance.

Stevens continues with section 602 of the Act explaining in part, "it 'authorizes and directs' all federal departments and agencies empowered to extend federal financial assistance to issue 'rules, regulations, or orders of general applicability' in order to 'effectuate' section 601's antidiscrimination mandate" (303). Stevens derides the majority's stance that each of the statute's sections operate in isolation. Stevens makes clear the statutory language does not suggest that the courts are supposed to place the provisions of the statute into two separate categories depending on how the courts believe the regulations track to the text of section 601. For Stevens, section 602 of the statute is aimed directly at ensuring the agency can implement the antidiscrimination requirements of section 601. Moreover, according to Stevens the Court has long held that this particular statute has allowed agencies to issue "prophylactic rules aimed at realizing the vision" for the statute, "even if the conduct capture by these rules is at times broader than that which would otherwise be prohibited" (305).

The dissent places emphasis on section 602 of the statute which authorizes the agency to "effectuate" the law. In short, Stevens explains the plain meaning of the text (despite the majority's opinion otherwise) is that section 602 "provides the relevant agencies with sufficient authority to transform the statute's broad aspiration into social reality" (306). The critical difference for the dissenting opinion is made clear when Stevens explains the agency's regulations "apply" the statutes prohibition on discrimination generally and not just the intentional discrimination that carries private enforceability through section 601. The dissent argues the Court should give weight to the "effects" regulation put forth by the agency, as in this case the agency's "considered judgment" may help ameliorate discriminatory practices of federal contractors. Taking a page from Scalia's book that seemingly calls for *Chevron* deference whenever possible, Stevens explains

Chevron deference applies when, "...Congress has clearly delegated agencies the power to issue regulations with the force of law and established formal procedures for the promulgation of such regulations" (309). Unlike Scalia, the dissent has no trouble finding the statute as calling for the courts to defer to agency discretion as outlined in this case.

For the purposes of this project, it is relevant to note that the dissenting opinion also relied in part on legislative history. Stevens includes remarks from Representative Lindsay introducing an amendment as well as statements from Attorney General Kennedy during the Senate and House Judiciary Committee meetings as evidence of the broad discretionary powers Congress intended for the agency. By referencing prior cases, the dissent also reiterates that in an effort to understand Congressional intent in the past the Court has, "...examined the nature of the rights at issue, the text and structure of the statute, and the relevant *legislative history*" (emphasis added, 312), thus taking issue with Scalia's description of legislative history as borderline illegitimate.

Oregon

The next case *Oregon* 546 U.S. 243 (2006) was a controversy regarding the powers afforded the Attorney General and whether his decision to overturn an Oregon law authorizing physicians to prescribe controlled substances to terminally ill patients was permissible under the Controlled Substances Act (CSA). Specifically, the Attorney General issued the following interpretive rule stating,

> assisting suicide is not a legitimate medical purpose within the meaning of 21 CFR 1306.04 (2001), and that prescribing, dispensing, or administering federally controlled substances to assist suicide violates the Controlled Substances Act. Such conduct by a physician registered to dispense controlled substances may render his registration . . . inconsistent with the public interest and therefore subject to possible suspension or revocation under 21 U. S. C. 824(a)(4).

The state of Oregon, (as well as a pharmacist, physician and terminally ill patients) argued to the District Court for the district of Oregon that the interpretive rule was impermissible and the District Court placed a permanent injunction against the enforcement of the rule. The US Court of Appeals for the Ninth Circuit determined the rule was invalid, primarily due to the 10th amendment, explaining the rule altered the constitutional balance between the states and federal government. The Supreme Court granted the governments petition for certiorari and Stevens wrote a 6-3 majority opinion (joined by Breyer) affirming the Court of Appeals. Scalia wrote a dissenting opinion.

Stevens begins by explaining *Auer* deference is not permissible in this case given the agency rule, "does little more than restate the terms of the statute itself" (244). Recall that under *Auer*, the Court held that agencies are entitled deference for interpreting rules an agency promulgates, so long as the interpretation of those rules are not "plainly erroneous or inconsistent with the regulation." Stevens explains that the key phrases at issue in the statute such as "medical purpose," "valid prescription," and "in the course of professional practice" are rehashed in the Attorney General's rule, but the rule itself does not clarify the statute. Stevens explains, "an agency does not acquire special authority to interpret its own words when, instead of using its expertise and experience to formulate a regulation, it has elected merely to paraphrase the statutory language" (244). After establishing that *Auer* is not relevant, Stevens also determines *Chevron* deference is not owed to the agency in this case to interpret the CSA, because the "CSA does not grant the Attorney General this broad authority to promulgate rules" (259). In other words, Stevens is invoking the precedent established in *Mead* which distinguished *Chevron* by first requiring Congress to show it delegated authority to the agency generally to make rules carrying the force of law. Stevens' reading of the CSA finds that the Attorney General does not provide the authority to promulgate any and all rules as related to the CSA, but only rules related to "registration" and "control" and "for the efficient execution of his functions" as stipulated by the CSA. Stevens addresses each of the quoted phrases above in turn to show how the Attorney General's interpretive rule does not fit within any of those categories.

To the first point regarding "registration," Stevens explains the related statutory language, as amended, allows the Attorney General to deny an applicant's registration, "if he determines that the issuance of such registration would be inconsistent with the public interest" (261). Moreover, the CSA requires that the Attorney General consider five factors as a way to assess "public interest," including the State's recommendation; compliance with state, federal, and local laws regarding controlled substances; and public health and safety, none of which were attempted by the Attorney General prior to the interpretive rule. Stevens also notes that the interpretive rule makes the issuing of drugs for the purpose of assisted suicide a federal crime and that authority is well beyond the Attorney General's statutory authority to register (and deregister).

To the second point concerning "control," Stevens explains that this term is in a subsection of the CSA which defines how the Attorney General can schedule drugs and substances. However, the scheduling powers afforded to the Attorney General require that scheduling decisions are made on the record and undergo rulemaking procedures as defined by the APA. Given the Attorney General did not employ such rulemaking procedures, the argument that the Attorney General has this power under the "control" provisions of the statute also fails.

To the third point concerning the phrase, "for the efficient execution of his functions" Stevens notes the statutory powers are shared by both the Attorney General and the Secretary of Health and Human Services. For example, the Attorney General cannot add, remove, or reschedule substances without first consulting with the Secretary of Health and Human Services findings on "scientific and medical matters." Stevens explains that the shared statutory powers with the Secretary of Health and Human Services weigh against the idea that the CSA permits the Attorney General to put forth rules that are quintessentially medical in nature.

Finally, the majority opinion reiterates the holding of the lower courts' 10th Amendment concerns by explaining that the CSA is premised on, "functioning medical profession regulated under the States" (270). According to Stevens, the Attorney General's jurisdiction is limited given the substantive role the States have regarding medicine generally. For example, Stevens points out that under the CSA, The Attorney General "can register a physician to dispense controlled substances if the applicant is authorized to dispense . . . controlled substances under the laws of the State in which he practices" (270). Moreover, the Attorney General must consider "the recommendation of the appropriate state licensing board..." when determining whether to revoke a physician's registration.

Before covering Scalia's dissent, first a quick note on Thomas's very brief dissenting opinion. Thomas's separate opinion is squarely aimed at pointing out the Court's reversal on the scope and purpose of the CSA as related to a case decided only 7 months previous in *Gonzales v. Raich*, 545 U. S. (2005).[14] According to Thomas, in that case the majority held that the CSA is a comprehensive regulatory regime designed to regulate controlled substances that can be utilized for medicinal purposes and in what manner. In addition, Thomas points out that the majority opinion, "concluded that the 'manner' in which controlled substances can be utilized 'for medicinal purpose' is one of the core activities regulated by the CSA" (299).

Thomas explains that the majority's decision is puzzling insofar it is "based in no small part on the structure and limitations of federalism" giving power to the states to regulate this issue, the very opposite position the majority held in *Gonzales v. Raich* which broadly interpreted the CSA to authorize federal supremacy over state laws in that case. Thomas's critique is especially relevant given Scalia voted with the majority in that case. Keeping that in mind, we turn to Scalia's dissent next.

Scalia begins his dissent by claiming there are three primary reasons the majority opinion is wrong to overrule the Attorney General's interpretive rule. First, the Attorney General's interpretation of "legitimate medical purpose" is valid and deserving of *Auer* deference, whereby the court defers to an agency interpretation of an ambiguous regulation. Second, even if the Court determines *Auer* deference is not owed, the Court should still uphold the interpretation as the Attorney General employs the most reasonable interpretation of the regulatory language anyway. In other words, assuming *Auer* deference is not owed, the Court judging the interpretation de novo (i.e., anew or for the first time) should still result in the conclusion that the agency interpretation is valid from the regulatory language alone. Third, the Attorney General should be afforded *Chevron* deference regarding the agency's interpretation of the CSA's statutory terms "public interest" and the implicit interpretation of the statutory phrase "public health and safety" given they are reasonable and authoritative.

Scalia employs his literalist method of interpretation to show that the Attorney General's rule does in fact clarify the statute by offering a definition for "prescription." For Scalia, the agency's adoption of a narrow definition for prescription that is objectively focused on a "legitimate medical purpose," distinguishes the statute and adds clarity as regulations often seek to accomplish. Scalia cites Webster's dictionary in support of the agency definition adopted. Scalia continues by explaining the definition adopted by the agency is not only reasonable, but the most natural interpretation by showing medical purpose as legitimate in relation to federal law. Scalia takes issue with the majority's understanding of the word "controlling" as used in the statute. According to Scalia, the definition employed by the majority opinion does not apply across the entire regulation, but only part of the regulation dealing with manufacturing, distribution, and dispensing of substances, none of which apply to the scheduling of drugs—the limiting function given to the Attorney General by the majority. Instead, Scalia explains the intention of "control" in the relevant statutory text in question was intended to embody the ordinary meaning of the term. Scalia once again cites a dictionary to show control as meaning, "to exercise, restrain or direct influence over; to dominate; regulate; hence, to hold from action; to curb." Using this definition, Scalia contends that the Attorney General's interpretation of the prescription requirement fits with the regulatory language, "…control of the . . . dispensing of controlled substances" because prescriptions are the primary mechanism to dispense drugs. In short, Scalia's literalist analysis results in the opposite conclusion that the Attorney General has interpretive authority relating to the registration and control of the manufacture, distribution, and dispensing of controlled substances.

Scalia continues by explaining the statutory language "public interest" is especially ambiguous and necessarily requires broad discretion to effectuate in practice. According to statute, the Attorney General "may refuse to register or deregister if he determines that registration is inconsistent with the public interest." Scalia notes (majority also agrees with this point) that the broad terms were part of the amended legislation's larger attempt to empower the agency to have discretion over registration from the decisions of state authorities. Scalia contends that in regards to registration and deregistration, the

Attorney General is solely charged with implementing the regulation and thus has implicit authority from Congress to define and implement such broad statutory terms. Scalia notes that even under the precedent set in *Mead*—which distinguished *Chevron* by requiring Congress indicate the agency was intended to promulgate rules—the court does not require an "explicit" delegation of rulemaking authority.

For Scalia, the statute clearly gives implicit authority to the agency to promulgate rules clarifying the authorizing statute, and according to *Chevron*, "...a court may not substitute its own construction of a statutory provision for a reasonable interpretation made by the administrator of an agency." Scalia continues by noting that even if explicit delegation were required, the regulations regarding registration clearly show such rulemaking authority was given under the provision stating in part, the Attorney General will, "...promulgate rules and regulations . . . relating to the registration and control of the manufacture, distribution, and dispensing of controlled substances."

Scalia takes issue with the majority's stance on the structure of the statute as reason to believe that Congress did not intend for the agency to promulgate rules regarding public interest at large. Recall, the majority opinion explained the Secretary of Health and Human Service is responsible for scientific and medical determinations. In response to this argument Scalia points out the Secretary is not mentioned at all within the registration provisions of the statute. Moreover, the scheduling of drugs is not "exclusive, or even primarily" related to medical and scientific factors, but encompasses all the "policy goals and competing enforcement priorities that attend any exercise of prosecutorial discretion" (296). Scalia argues that it would make sense that Congress thought it easier to have the Attorney General make some limited medical judgments as opposed to having the Secretary of Health and Human Services enforce police powers. Scalia also makes the claim that the decision of whether assisted suicide is permissible does not depend on science or medical determinations, but is merely a "naked value judgment," and that, "If legitimate medical purpose has any meaning, it surely excludes the prescription of drugs to produce death" (299).

Finally, in response to the majority's claim that the Attorney General does not have authority to promulgate criminal sanctions under the statute, Scalia cites the regulations and emphasizes that it is reasonable to conclude that those acts not in "compliance with applicable . . . Federal . . . laws relating to controlled substances" and "threaten the public health and safety" to suffer penalties. Moreover, Scalia shows the penalty clause includes soft and conditional language. For example, "*...possible* suspension", and "*may* render his resignation..." (emphasis added) as reasonable consequences for doctors ignoring the law.

Scalia's deference to the agency in this case was offered through the textual interpretation he applied along with a seemingly bright line approach of deference to agencies for any statutory and regulatory ambiguity (regardless of outcome). Although the extent to which consequences impacted Scalia's decision is ultimately unknown, it is worth noting that Scalia did offer the example that Congress's position on the structure of how the Attorney General and Secretary of Health and Human Service operate was reasonable based on his own hypothetical.

---

[14]The Court held in *Gonzales v. Raich* that Congress was permitted under the commerce clause to prohibit the local cultivation and use of marijuana—validating the CSA—despite California's law allowing medicinal use of marijuana. Justice Breyer and Scalia voted with the majority in that case.

CHAPTER 7
Judging the Judges

> Absolute discretion, like corruption, marks the beginning of the end of liberty.
> —Justice Douglas William, *New York v. United States*

OVERVIEW

This chapter begins the analysis of Scalia's and Breyer's jurisprudence and the effects of their opinions on public administration and administrative discretion particularly. The first half of this chapter categorizes a number of factors related to each Justice's opinions. The goal here is to capture any discernible themes of Breyer's and Scalia's jurisprudence. Those themes are then highlighted by detailing examples from the case opinions to show how each Justice's methods of legal reasoning and statutory interpretation attempt to draw boundaries regarding the limits of administrative discretion. Tables 7.1-7.4 (discussed more below) answers the following descriptive and evaluative questions for each case reviewed:

1. Did the Justice's decision defer or overrule the federal agency action or interpretation under review;
2. Did the decision empower or constrain the agency's regulatory powers;
3. Did the opinion cite legislative history to support the decision;
4. Did the opinion rely on or emphasize agency procedures as part of the decision;

5. Did the opinion emphasize the practical consequence(s) that would result from decision or the legislative purpose;
6. Did the opinion broadly or narrowly interpret the statute/regulation in question;

Although some judgment was required on part of the researcher to successfully capture the above characteristics for each opinion reviewed, this aspect of qualitative research is also its greatest strength. For example, the case study review allows the researcher to get beyond the overarching decision of the Court and attempt to understand the approach and method of legal reasoning embodied by the opinion. In other words, each opinion was carefully analyzed with respect to the above criteria to reasonably assess the extent to which each element listed above influenced the Judge's opinion. Answering these questions helps organize the many factors associated with legal reasoning to give the research findings some practical applications for public administrators. The categorization of each Judge's decision with respect to above criteria is foremost derived from the language of the opinions directly; however, taking a collective view that factors all 19 cases reviewed (all of which focus on administrative discretion), along with the knowledge of the literature and extra-juridical writings for each Justice's approach to the law, allows the researcher to do what administrators are called to do by the courts on occasions when ambiguity arises, and utilize some judgment and discretion! That said, a description regarding how the analysis answered each of the descriptive and evaluative questions are discussed next.

The first descriptive question is whether the Judge deferred to the agency position or overruled the agency action or interpretation. It is important to note the analysis captures each Judge's deference to the *federal* agency's position and not the position of any state, county, or local governmental agency that may also be associated with the case. For example, in *Harris County*, Breyer's dissent does not defer to the state agency's position on administering English only drivers license tests, but does defer to the DOL's position that individuals have actionable rights to challenge and thus enforce federal agency regulations. In this case, the research categorizes Breyer as deferring to the agency, as once again, the analysis is focused on deference to federal agencies.

The second question regarding whether the Judge's decision empowers or constrains the regulatory reach of the agency is distinguished from the first question and used as a separate category because the answers to both question are not necessarily the same. For example, Breyer's dissent in *Massachussets* disagreed with the EPA's position to *not* regulate greenhouse gases. Although Breyer did not defer to the agency position, Breyer's dissent was calling for more administrative authority and regulatory jurisdiction, thus his decision is categorized as empowering the agency.

The third question reviewed documents any instances whereby the Justice cites legislative history as part of the rationale for their decision. Legislative history can include a range of factors including, Senate and House committee reports, Representative and Senator statements, as well as agency officials describing the purpose or intent of the bill or statute during Congressional meetings. Instances where the opinion cites failed bills or amendments as evidence of the intent of the statute in question are also included. The analysis will record for each Justice any use of legislative history as cited from members of the Court the Justice voted with as well.

The fourth question is focused on whether the Justice placed any emphasis on the agency's procedures or lack thereof. In other words, the analysis takes into account any statements from the Justice (or members of the Court the Justice voted with) that suggest the agency's use, or failure to use procedures affected the Judge's decision. For example, if the Justice's opinion makes note of the agency's decision to undergo notice-and-comment rulemaking or contrarily notes an agency's failure to provide opportunity for public participation (e.g., interpretive rule) as part of their argument, these potential concerns were recorded.

The fifth question asks whether the Judge's decision places some emphasis on the consequence or effects of the decision in the future. In other words, did the opinion include language indicating the likely effects or external considerations were a central element to the decision? This question is not focused on the particular legal effects resultant from the opinion as this is an unavoidable consequence for any legal decision. Instead, the analysis will look for statements suggesting the Justice was concerned with any external or larger macro-effects on the citizenry, private business, or regulatory agencies, etc. For example, Scalia's comment in *Babbit*, explaining the majority opinion, "imposes unfairness to the point of financial ruin…" regarding business-owners affected by the ESA, suggests some amount of concern for the external or macro-consequence of the decision was a factor for the decision—beyond just a reading of the statute or regulation in isolation. The concept of legislative purpose (e.g., what interpretation best fits with the larger aim or purpose of the law and/or regulatory history) is also included in the categorization of consequence, as this concept is very similar to a Judge's decision to consider the practical consequence of a decision. With that in mind, any evidence of the decision invoking either one of these factors (legislative purpose or consequence) was categorized as such.

The sixth question reviewed examined textual interpretation. Although a few cases reviewed seemed to indicate whether the Justices' interpretation was rooted in "originalism" or "intentionalism," it was too difficult to categorize all of the decisions as such with any degree of confidence. Primarily this is so because the language used to describe the texts were normally portraying the precision of the text and less so what it meant at the time it was drafted (originalism) or how a fictional member of Congress would give meaning to the text (intentionalism). For example, the descriptive language included terms such as, "fair reading," "non-ambiguous," "permissible," "plain meaning," or "on its face." However, these descriptions are not necessarily helpful to distinguish the methods of statutory interpretations described above. To account for this problem, the analysis was broadened to evaluate whether the interpretation embodied by each Justice was simply broad or narrow. Answering this question also required some level of judgment on part of the researcher. However, to minimize subjectivity, the categorization of "broad" or "narrow" was assigned with respect to how the dissent and majority opinions differed. For example, if Scalia's interpretation of the statute was narrower than opposing Justices' reading of the statute, then his decision is categorized as "narrow" and vice versa for "broad."

The results of the analysis are shown in Tables 7.1-7.4. Each table lists the cases in chronological order (the same order they were also presented in chapters 3-6), and categorizes the results for each of the descriptive and evaluative questions described above for both Justices. The tables are separated by the corresponding chapters each case was discussed. Tables 7.5 is a summary table condensing all of the opinions reviewed in this project for each Justice separately.

Table 7.1 Analysis of SEC, FDA, and FCC Cases

Case Name	Broad or Narrow	Defer to Agency Position	Increase Regulatory Power	Legislative History	Consequence or Legislative Purpose	Agency Procedure
United States v. O'Hagan (1997)						
Breyer	Broad	Yes	Yes	No	Yes	No
Scalia	Narrow	No	No	No	Yes	No
FDA v. Brown (2000)						
Breyer	Broad	Yes	Yes	No	Yes	No
Scalia	Narrow	No	No	Yes	No	No
FCC v. Fox (2009)						
Breyer	Narrow	No	No	No	Yes	No
Scalia	Broad	Yes	Yes	Yes	No	No
Talk America Inc. v. Michigan (2011)						
Breyer	Broad	Yes	Yes	No	No	No
Scalia	Broad	Yes	Yes	No	No	No
City of Arlington v. FCC (2013)[15]						
Breyer	Broad	Yes	Yes	Yes	Yes	No
Scalia	Narrow	Yes	Yes	No	Yes	No

Table 7.2 Analysis of EPA Cases

Case Name	Broad or Narrow	Defer to Agency Position	Increase Regulatory Power	Legislative History	Consequence or Legislative Purpose	Agency Procedure
Babbitt v. Sweet Home (1995)						
Breyer	Broad	Yes	Yes	Yes	Yes	No
Scalia	Narrow	No	No	Yes	Yes	No
Norton v. Southern Utah Wilderness Alliance (2004)						
Breyer	Narrow	Yes	Yes	No	Yes	No
Scalia	Narrow	Yes	Yes	No	Yes	No
MA. v. EPA[16] (2007)						
Breyer	Broad	No	Yes	No	No	No
Scalia	Narrow	Yes	Yes	No	No	No
National Association of Homebuilder v. Defenders of Wildlife (2007)						
Breyer	Broad	No	Yes	Yes	Yes	No
Scalia	Narrow	Yes	No	No	No	Yes
Coeur Alaska, Inc. v. Southeast Alaska Conservation Council[17] (2009)						
Breyer	Broad	Yes	Yes	No	Yes	Yes
Scalia	Broad	Yes	Yes	No	Yes	Yes
Utility Air Regulatory Group v. EPA (2014)						
Breyer	Broad	Yes	Yes	Yes	Yes	No
Scalia	Narrow	No	No	No	No	No

Table 7.3 Analysis of DOL Cases

Case Name	Broad or Narrow	Defer to Agency Position	Increase Regulatory Power	Legislative History	Consequence or Legislative Purpose	Agency Procedure
Christensen v. Harris County (2000)						
Breyer	Broad	Yes	Yes	No	No	No
Scalia	Narrow	No	No	No	No	No
Christopher v. SmithKline Beecham Corp. (2012)						
Breyer	Narrow	Yes	Yes	No	No	No
Scalia	Broad	No	No	No	Yes	Yes
Long Island Care at Home LTD., v. Coke (2007)						
Breyer	Broad	Yes	Yes	No	Yes	Yes
Scalia	Broad	Yes	Yes	No	Yes	Yes
Perez, v. Mortgage Bankers Association (2015)						
Breyer	Narrow	Yes	Yes	No	Yes	No
Scalia	Narrow	Yes	Yes	No	Yes	No

Table 7.4 Analysis of IRS and DOJ Cases

Case Name	Broad or Narrow	Defer to Agency Position	Increase Regulatory Power	Legislative History	Consequence or Legislative Purpose	Agency Procedure
United States v. Fior D'Italia, Inc. (2002)						
Breyer	Broad	Yes	Yes	No	No	No
Scalia	Narrow	No	No	No	Yes	No
Alexander v. Sandoval (2001)						
Breyer	Broad	Yes	Yes	Yes	Yes	No
Scalia	Narrow	No	No	No	No	Yes
Gonzales v. Oregon (2006)						
Breyer	Narrow	No	No	No	Yes	Yes
Scalia	Broad	Yes	Yes	No	Yes	No
United States v. Mead (2001)						
Breyer	Narrow	No	No	No	No	Yes
Scalia	Broad	Yes	Yes	No	Yes	No

Table 7.5 Summary of Scalia and Breyer Opinions Reviewed

Justice	Broad	Narrow	Defer to Agency Position	Increase Regulatory Power	Legislative History	Consequence or Legislative Purpose	Agency Procedure
Breyer	68% (13/19)	32% (6/19)	74% (14/19)	84% (16/19)	26% (5/19)	68% (13/19)	21% (4/19)
Scalia	37% (7/19)	63% (12/19)	58% (11/19)	53% (10/19)	16% (3/19)	58% (11/19)	26% (5/19)

---

[15]Although Breyer voted with Scalia to enable the FCC to determine jurisdiction, Breyer caveated that regulatory power with his concurring opinion in support of *Mead*, and is therefore scored a "No" for "Increase Regulatory Power" category in comparison to Scalia's seemingly unlimited support of *Chevron* deference in this case.

[16]The categorization "Yes" was applied to the "Increase Regulatory Power" category for both Justices in this case, but for different reasons. Scalia's dissent argued that agency's should be able to use discretion for reasons outside of the statute (thus empowering agencies' discretionary/regulatory power) whereas

Breyer calls for the EPA to revisit its decision to not regulate greenhouse gases, suggesting Breyer's view is for the EPA to take on increased regulatory responsibility in the future.

[17]The categorization "Yes" was applied to the "Increase Regulatory Power" category for both Justices in regards to the Corp's permitting powers, and not the EPA's permitting power (which was reduced to some extent by the decision) as the Corp's discretionary power was most central to the case.

CHAPTER 8

Comparing Judicial Principles with Decisions

The Court's literalism is selective, and it results in a strange and disjointed regulatory scheme
—Justice Alito, *Utility Air Regulatory Group v. EPA*
...it is not illegal to run afoul of the 'purpose' of a statute, only its letter
—Justice Thomas, *United States v. O'Hagan*

IDENTIFYING AND APPLYING THEMES

This chapter begins the analysis of the opinions with respect to Table 7.1–7.4 findings, to discuss themes identified across all cases reviewed. To help construct this section of the analysis, Rohr's pillars (dialectic, pertinent, institutional, and concrete)—explaining the importance of assessing the judiciary as a way to assess "regime values"—are used as a guidepost to cover the opinions. The first section covers Rohr's "dialectic" pillar by exploring the consistency of each Justice's judicial review of administrative discretion and evaluates any apparent contradictions or disconnections from each Justice's stated theory of legal reasoning and actual practice. This section will also highlight key areas of agreement and disagreement between each Justice's opinions and the reasoning employed for their similar and contrary positions. The next section will use Rohr's "pertinent" pillar by focusing on how each Justice applied judicial review across different types of administrative actions found in the cases reviewed—all of which are relevant and important as they represent different methods practitioners actually use discretion. The types of discretion found in the cases reviewed include, agency notice-and-comment rulemaking, interpretive rules, interpretation of statutes, and agency inaction. In other words, this section groups the cases by different types of administrative actions to showcase how these varying actions were viewed by each Justice and how discretion was constrained or enabled. Finally, Rohr's pillars ("institutional" and "concrete") are combined to assess the impact of the opinions rendered by Scalia and Breyer on administrative agencies and the Court itself. For example, how do their opinions instruct public administrators on the topic of administrative discretion as well as divide power among the executive and legislative branches? The "institutional" lens is used in this section as well to a much lesser extent, but is included to point out a few instances whereby each Justice's decision affected the institutional voice of the Court at large by setting the groundwork for future cases or dramatically changing past precedent.

Dialectic

A view of the dialectic discussion between Scalia's and Breyer's jurisprudence was readily assessable as the Justices were on opposite sides of the Court for 13 of the 19 cases reviewed. This amount of disagreement between the two Justices on the topic of administrative law was somewhat surprising, even despite the many factors discussed in chapter 2 explaining their differing approaches to the role of Judge. This rate of disagreement might be expected for a review of more predictable/political issues such as 1st amendment or commerce clause cases, but it was interesting to find the administrative law cases generated such varied opinions given their shared background and interest in administrative law. Of the six cases whereby their votes did align, four of those instances were unanimous opinions (i.e., *Coke*, *Norton*, *Talk America Inc.* and *Perez*), suggesting perhaps those cases did not offer much opportunity for a Judge to deviate from case precedent, or the legal questions were altogether less controversial. The only opinions they both joined when the Court itself was divided was the *Coeur Alaska, Inc.* and *City of Arlington* decisions. Yet, even in those decisions, Scalia and Breyer write separately to explain their differing views on how *Chevron* should be applied by the courts. Thus, the *Chevron* deference theme is the first point of dialectic discussion discussed next, as this theme was paramount and influenced many of the opinions reviewed.

First, it is no surprise that judicial deference to agency decisions was debated often as the case selections were focused on administrative discretion. Thus, almost every case reviewed included citations to important Court cases that explain the amount of deference owed to agencies under different scenarios. Namely, the Court routinely cited *Skidmore, Chevron, Mead,* and *Auer* to either support their position not to defer to the agency, or to support their decision to defer to the agency position, depending on the specifics of the case and how the particular agency actions met the Justice's view of deference owed under those above cases. To some extent, each Justice's rhetoric regarding judicial review of administrative discretion does not produce the kinds of opinions one would expect to find.

For example, Scalia goes beyond citations and takes up focused discussions on judicial review and deference owed to agencies in five of the cases reviewed (*Coeur Alaska, Inc., Harris County, Mead*, and *Talk America Inc.* and *City of Arlington*). In each of these cases, Scalia gives similar reasons with varying emphasis on why the *Chevron* deference principal should continue to serve as the primary model for judicial review, despite the distinguishing precedent set in *Mead.* Namely, Scalia emphasizes the practical advantage of applying *Chevron* deference in each of these cases. For instance, Scalia makes clear in *Coeur Alaska, Inc.,* that a, "vast body of complex laws committed to the charge of executive agencies" requires some assurance the courts will "accept reasonable and authoritative agency interpretation of ambiguous provisions" (296). Although Breyer does not specifically take on the discussion of applying *Chevron* deference in this case, he does join the opinion with Scalia, and in his separate concurring opinion also makes note of the regulatory complexity facing administrators. Breyer explains the agency's permitting decision reflects, "…the kind of detailed decision that the *statutes delegate* authority to the EPA…" (emphasis added 294). However, it is this point of "statutory delegation" that captures the primary source of Breyer's and Scalia's disagreement on the amount of deference owed to agency interpretation of statutes from a theoretical standpoint.

For Breyer, the courts must first determine if Congress intended the agency to have discretionary power over the action/interpretation in question. Whereas Scalia holds than any ambiguity in a statute post *Chevron*, requires the courts to assume Congress intended the agency to fill-in any statutory gaps and reasonably interpret and effectuate the statute. This point of contrast was detailed further in the *Harris County* opinion whereby Scalia and Breyer write separate opinions targeting each other to explain the difference of when and how *Chevron* deference applies. Once again, Breyer stresses that under *Mead*, the courts must determine if the statute implicitly assigned discretionary power to the agency or did not and Scalia explains the only questions for the court regarding whether to apply *Chevron* deference is to determine whether the agency position is authoritative, if the statute is in fact ambiguous, and if the agency did attempt to interpret the statute. If the answer is no for any of these questions, then courts are right not to apply deference. In short, although both Justices give some weight to the practical need of administrative expertise to solve technical and sophisticated regulatory problems, Breyer's theoretical argument reserves a role for the courts to check administrative discretion by questioning whether Congress intended for broad delegation of powers for agencies on a case by case basis and Scalia draws a theoretical line in the sand for courts to assume all ambiguous statutes are to be resolved by the agency. Yet, each Justices' theoretical accounting of deference does not clearly match the opinions rendered across all cases, discussed next.

Scalia's bright line approach would seemingly result in considerable deference afforded to agency decisions, whereas Breyer's calling for courts to determine if Congress intended agency discretion would suggest less deference. However, the case review revealed that Breyer actually deferred to the agency position more often than Scalia. Breyer deferred to the agency in 14 of 19 cases, whereas Scalia only deferred 11 of 19 times. Similarly, Breyer's decisions granted the agency more regulatory authority in 16 of 19 cases, whereas Scalia only did so in 10 of 19 cases reviewed. One possible explanation for the difference could be their method of statutory interpretation which was captured here as broad or narrow. Breyer employed a broader reading of the statute/regulation than Scalia, with a 68% to 37% rate of such interpretation respectively. In all 13 cases that Breyer offered a broad interpretation of the statute, the decision also empowered the agency's regulatory power. Similarly, 11 of those decisions utilizing a broad interpretation also deferred to the agency position. Breyer only applied a narrow reading to the statute in 6 cases, and only 3 of those narrow readings deferred to the agency position and increased the agency's regulatory power.

A review of Scalia's method of interpretation produced similar results. Scalia applied a broad interpretation of the statute for 7 of the cases with 6 of those decisions resulting in deference and increased regulatory power to the agency. Thus in only 5 instances did Scalia's narrow interpretation of the statute empower the agency's regulatory power, and in only 4 instances did the narrow reading defer to the agency position. Although it is difficult to determine if Scalia attempted to apply his method of literalism to statutory interpretation across all cases (hence the decision to categorize broad and narrow readings instead) a review of the cases does give some insight regarding the extent to which Scalia was faithful to this approach.

Discussed first are some examples that suggest Scalia veered from literalism to some degree. On two occasions Justice Thomas (who also endorses literalism) criticized Scalia's interpretations as purposive and inconsistent with the wording of the statutory text. For example, in *O'Hagan* Thomas notes the majority opinion (which Scalia joined) takes a "purposive" approach by going far beyond the words of the statute. Similarly, Thomas points out the majority opinion in *Gonzales v. Raich* (joined by Scalia) gives a very broad and purposive view of the CSA, and Scalia's dissent in *Oregon* is consistent in that regard as it also calls for a broad reading of the CSA. Although Thomas's dissent was really directed at the majority's shift from *Gonzales v. Raich*, (broad reading of the CSA) to *Oregon*, (narrow reading of the CSA), it was still interesting that Scalia did not take up the argument of whether his opinions in both cases were rooted in purpose as opposed to text as Thomas alleged, perhaps giving some validity to the criticism. Similarly confusing though was Breyer's decision to not take up the argument at all given Breyer was a part of the majority in both cases and was thus the subject of Thomas's criticism that the Court was enabling the Department of Justice in one case and constraining the agency in the latter case based on different readings of the same statutory language.

The best case evidencing Scalia most likely did not adhere to literalism was found in the review of *Christopher*. In this case, it was Breyer who made a compelling literalist argument as to the meaning of "outside salesman" by relying on historic documents such as the DOL

Wage and Hour Division's 1949 report that defined "company representative" to show how salesman and representatives were understood during the time the regulatory terms were adopted. The fact that the legal pragmatist Breyer was applying such a literalist framework as the primary mode of argumentation was to some extent surprising given his rhetoric, but even more-so was the majority opinion (joined by Scalia) which actually de-emphasized these historical references. In this case it was Breyer who criticized the majority as going beyond the statute and giving the text "special meaning" to reach a broader purpose. In addition, the DOL filed an amicus brief in this case explaining Breyer's textual argument was correct and that pharmaceutical detailers are non-exempt employees. Recall in *Harris County,* Scalia explains one of the prongs for determining whether *Chevron* deference is applicable is based on whether the agency gives an authoritative stance on the matter. In that case Scalia specifically explained the amicus brief co-signed by the Solicitor of Labor served as the agency's authoritative position, but yet in the *Christopher* case, the amicus brief is ignored by the majority. It is hard to imagine that Scalia applied a literalist approach given Breyer's detailed literalist argument in support of the contrary position, along with the authoritative stance of the agency via the amicus brief affirming Breyer's interpretation was essentially ignored by Scalia. If the amicus brief were given any weight, then according to Scalia's theoretical accounting of deference, the application of *Chevron* was warranted and thus only a reasonable agency-interpretation of the statute was necessary. As described in chapter 5, it is more likely the majority opinion employed a consequentialist approach by stressing the economic effects the decision would have on the pharmaceutical industry, an approach that better aligns with Breyer's said practice of emphasizing consequences over literalism.

The above examples suggest Scalia was not resolute in his application of literalism; however, some other cases offer support that a literalist approach was applied. For example, in *National Association of Homebuilders,* and *Babbitt* the opinion cited dictionaries published near the time the statutes were passed to define statutory terms, resulting in a narrow reading of the authorizing legislation. Similarly, in *Oregon* Scalia used a dictionary to show the Attorney General's definition of the term "prescription" as valid and proper to the extent it clarified the authorizing statute. In other cases Scalia seemed to emphasize a literalist reading of the statute by giving ample descriptions of the meaning of words and canons of construction to derive the proper meaning from the text. For example, in *Massachusetts* Scalia explains the term "air pollutant" as narrowly defined by the agency was reasonable and thus actionable. Similarly, Scalia explains in *Sandoval* the search for congressional intent was found, "with the text and structure" of the statute alone.

Although the opinions reviewed do not indicate Scalia uniformly applied literalism, it was apparent that Scalia at least gave more attention to the written language as measured by the length of descriptions his opinions used to explain how various terms applied or should be understood with respect to the statute/regulation. With this in mind, it is reasonable to conclude that to some extent his method of literalism was in the forefront of his decisions, and in most instances resulted in a narrow interpretation of the statutory language. Of course, the review of literalism here was limited to a review of Scalia's application of such interpretation, but Justice Thomas's is also of the literalist tradition and his opinions align with Scalia more often than any other two Justices on the Court, which also proved to be the case for this project as they voted together in 18 of the 19 cases. Thus, assuming Thomas also attempts to apply a literalist approach to the law and they voted together so often gives some weight that a literalist approach does in fact render narrower interpretations.

The research finding that literalism constrains rather than enables statutory interpretation is especially relevant for administrators who are charged with interpreting and implementing authorizing statutes. The research findings here indicate that a public administrator attempting to discern the original intent of the statutory language as understood by people during the time the statute was written will most likely result in the administrator deciding a narrowed view on the statutory language. This in turn, would most likely limit the amount of administrative discretion afforded under the statute and constrain administrative actions.

Breyer's jurisprudence indicated a close connection between his use of consequence and legislative purpose and the broad or narrow interpretation applied to the statute or regulation. In the 13 cases reviewed whereby Breyer's opinions supported a consequentialist or purposive approach to the law, 9 of those decisions also carried a broad interpretation of the statute. Similarly, the 13 cases using consequence or legislative purpose also deferred to the agency position 10 times, and moreover, strengthened the agency's regulatory power in 11 instances. However, it is Breyer's willingness to empower an agency's regulatory reach in 16 of the 19 cases reviewed that is most striking from the analysis, and in reverse, it could be his preference for agency resolution over judicial or congressional resolution that actually serves as the driving force behind the use of broad statutory interpretations, consequence, and legislative purpose. Although it is difficult to untangle precisely which factor is predominantly steering his decisions, Breyer does offer ample evidence in his opinions to support the notion that he prefers executive branch resolution to regulator problems, discussed next.

One of the themes found through analyzing Breyer opinions is a strong presumption in favor of executive resolution of administrative problems—as opposed to legislative or judicial—despite his rhetoric suggesting a strong judicial approach or check is required. For example, in *O'Hagan*, and *Coeur Alaska Inc.*, Breyer's position supports that agencies take on some inventiveness to solve regulatory issues that arise. Specifically, Breyer's decision to join the majority in *O'Hagan* supported the rationale that courts are correct to give some legal latitude to an agency's attempt to regulate real problems that likely occur on a regular basis. In this case, the SEC was attempting to prevent third parties from committing insider trading—a circumstance the majority opinion explained is commonplace given lawyers, investment bankers, and accountants oftentimes help structure large stockholder deals and gain foreknowledge of non-public information without having a fiduciary responsibility—by challenging the authorizing statute to apply a novel-criminal penalty.

Similarly, Breyer highlights his tendency for agency empowerment in *Fior D'Italia* when he reasons the IRS is right to seek remedies to potential tax loopholes through inventive tax levies. Breyer offers considerable leeway to the agency despite the financial effects this method will have on restaurants attempting to meet the new aggregate tax methodology developed by the IRS. In this case, Breyer's opinion is not rooted in an effort to ensure the IRS produces more accurate tax levies (namely because the IRS tax aggregate method does not account for FICA tax limits based on salary as pointed out by the dissent), but rather, places more concern on the agency's ability to efficiently address tax problems without having to resort to performing individual audits of wait staff. Breyer's decision allowing the tax levy to stand despite the likely effects of substantively higher tax levies on businesses is especially empowering to the IRS given the agency rule was not promulgated through notice-and-comment rulemaking, and thus there was no opportunity for businesses to challenge the new rule prior to its implementation. It is clear in this case that administrative efficiency and flexibility won the day over individual due process. Furthermore, Breyer makes the distinction of potential and actual administrative abuse in regards to the respondent's allegation that the IRS was abusing and coercing the new tax powers to convince businesses to sign-up for the agency's Tip Reporting Alternative Commitment program. For Breyer, the judiciary does not have a role in stopping potential administrative abuse, but deals only with actual abuse—a position which on its face would limit judicial review and empower agencies.

Breyer's calling for empowered regulatory agencies is best heard in his dissent in *Brown* and his decision to join the majority in *Massachusetts*. Recall in *Brown*, at issue was whether the FDA was authorized to regulate tobacco, and in *Massachusetts*, the question was whether the EPA was required to begin regulating greenhouse gases. Both of these were landmark administrative law cases that carried the potential to drastically change the scope of regulatory powers for the FDA and EPA respectively, as well as significantly impact the American economy financially. In both cases Breyer took the position it was the agency's responsibility for addressing the relevant issues. In the case of *Brown*, Breyer's dissenting opinion gives credence to the notion that he prefers administrative resolution of regulatory problems over and beyond the simple reliance on legislative history as a means to supporting Congress' intent and ultimately the decision. Specifically, Breyer finds room for broad discretionary powers within the authorizing statute alone and discounts the majority's emphasis on legislative history, competing statutes, and failed bills as reasons why the FDA should not regulate tobacco. In response to the majority's contention that the decision for FDA to regulate tobacco would necessarily result in a ban instead of mere regulations—a position even the FDA acknowledged as inappropriate—Breyer agrees with the agency's assessment that external-aggregate factors such as withdrawal symptoms and consumers moving towards more dangerous black market cigarettes are valid reasons for the agency to consider, supporting the agency's rationale to regulate and not ban tobacco outright. Breyer takes a functional approach to the statute by emphasizing the need for regulatory attention on the subject of tobacco given the increased scientific research supporting the FDA's position.

Scalia's decision to join the majority opinion in *Brown* which held it is inappropriate for agencies to base decisions on an external-aggregate analysis of all possible bad effects instead of the statute and legislative history is difficult to reconcile with the *Massachusetts* dissenting opinion he authored explaining that there is "no basis in law" for limiting agency discretion to statutory matters specifically. Recall, in *Massachusetts* Scalia was dissenting with the majority's decision to overturn the agency's position that climate change was a political issue and any regulatory action on the agency's part could inhibit the President's ability to negotiate with other countries to reduce emissions. Although Breyer agreed with the majority opinion in *Massachusetts* that the EPA could not factor something as remote as the President's foreign affairs as reason to not regulate greenhouse gas, his position in *Brown* which enables agencies to consider external-aggregate factors is not as inconsistent as Scalia. Namely, because the external-aggregate factors Breyer gives weight to in *Brown* flow directly from the statute, whereas Scalia calls for external considerations seemingly without limit in *Massachusetts*, and yet limits agency consideration of a very likely consequence (e.g., withdrawals, black market cigarettes) in *Brown*.

In addition to Breyer's tendency to enable administrative actions, he also gives evidence in various opinions that he is inclined to give a functional reading of the statutes to allow agencies to work. Similar to his book entitled, *Making Our Democracy Work: A Judge's View* whereby he calls for the courts to breathe life into the Constitution to keep it relevant, Breyer seems to offer broad or narrow interpretations to meet the needs of the overlying purpose of the agencies. For example, in *National Association of Homebuilders* Breyer took a functional approach towards the competing statutes by rendering an interpretation that allowed the ESA and the CWA to work together instead of in isolation. Breyer's separate dissenting opinion argues that the ESA requires all agencies to factor how their regulatory efforts may affect endangered species. Breyer gives the hypothetical example that if the FDA thought there was potential for the marketing of a new drug to impact the preservation or destruction of an endangered species, that under the ESA, the FDA would be required to confer with the EPA on the decision to authorize the use of such drugs. This view adds a nuance to the realm of factors Breyer holds as relevant for agency decision making discussed in *Brown* and *Massachusetts*, in that it goes beyond the agency's authorizing legislation, and allows for agency's to consider the authorizing legislation of *other* federal agencies.

Breyer takes the functionalist approach again in *Oregon*, calling for the Attorney General and Secretary of Health and Human Services to work together, thus rendering the Attorney General's attempt to uniformly control the definition and application of controlled drugs as impermissible. Breyer's majority-concurring opinion in *Coeur Alaska, Inc.*, also calls for a balanced and functional-regulatory approach by enabling the permitting powers of the Corps while also maintaining the regulatory power of the EPA. Instead of an all or nothing approach, Breyer works out an interpretation of the authorizing statute and regulations that allows the Corps to maintain its permitting powers while also enabling the EPA's role in overseeing the new source standard under the CWA. Breyer's functional approach was buttressed with his description of the administrative complexity concerning the varieties of discharges and effluent limitation regulations, giving more weight to the idea that Breyer is willing to eschew formalistic and literalist problems when possible to help agencies meet their regulatory demands.

The above themes are useful to revisit the central issue of discretion as discussed previously regarding whether and how to apply *Chevron* deference to administrative interpretations. Namely, it appears that Breyer's precautionary 1st step as understood through *Mead*, and reinforced in his separate concurring opinion in *City of Arlington,* requiring the judiciary reserve a role to determine if Congress implicitly intended administrative discretion for provisions of ambiguous statutes, is outweighed by a practical jurisprudence that supports agencies through a functional approach allowing substantial administrative leeway to interpret and regulate as necessary given the complicated regulatory environment. In contrast, Scalia's theoretical calling for the judiciary to defer to the agencies in most instances to ensure administrative flexibility and protect the separation of powers is significantly hindered by his literalist approach to statutory interpretation which results in a narrow interpretation of statutes that then forces him to intervene.

Interestingly, the role of legislative history played an insignificant role for both Justices. It was no surprise that Scalia did not emphasize legislative history given his theoretical position on the matter, but it was interesting to find that on one occasion (i.e., *Fox Television Inc.*,) Scalia authored his own opinion citing legislative history to help marshal his argument. It was also interesting that Scalia was not compelled to write a separate opinion distancing him from the very extensive legislative history offered up by Justice O'Connor's majority opinion in *Brown*, which by and large served as the primary factor that turned the case for the majority. Although Scalia brought forth an argument using legislative history in *Babbitt*, he first gave a disclaimer that legislative history is not a valid method of deciphering Congress' intent and was only presented to show how the majority opinion's use of legislative history (invalid methodology notwithstanding) was not in line with the legislative history that did exist for the case.

Similarly, Breyer's use of legislative history was unexpected. For instance, Breyer sidestepped the lengthy legislative history put forth in *Brown*, and instead opted to focus on the authorizing statutory language in isolation—a method one would expect for a literalist such as Scalia or Thomas. Most of all though, it was surprising to find that Breyer only cited legislative history in support of his opinions in 5 of the 19 cases reviewed, only 2 more times than Scalia's opinions referenced legislative history. The 5 citations came from *Sandoval, Babbitt, City of Arlington, Utility Air Regulatory Group,* and the *National Association of Homebuilders* cases. The *Sandoval* case involved the legislative history of the Civil Rights Act citing statements from the Attorney General during Senate and House Judiciary Committee meetings. The *Babbitt* and *National Association of Homebuilders* cases involved the legislative history of the ESA and Breyer's dissent in the *Utility Air Regulatory Group* considered the legislative history of the Clean Air Act. In *City of Arlington*, Breyer didn't necessarily use legislative history to decide the case, he does use the separate concurring opinion to reiterate that, "statutory purposes, including those revealed in part by legislative and regulatory history, can be similarly relevant..." to determine if *Chevron* deference is warranted. Although Breyer's use of legislative history was consistent in these cases, in each case Breyer's position also called for the agency to increase its regulatory powers, which as described above may have been the more central factor to his decision.

From an administrative perspective, the value of legislative history as seen from Scalia's, Breyer's, and the entire Court for that matter, did not amount to much. For starters, legislative history was only cited in 5 of the cases reviewed. Much more relevant for the Court was the statutory language at issue and the precedent(s) set from prior cases. Based on the cases reviewed here, an administrator's attempt to understand the legislative history may not get very far in trying to meet the aims of the statute and expectations of the courts. In addition to the limited attention legislative history received from the cases reviewed, the Justices were not always clear on how to interpret and use the legislative history when it was cited. For example, the majority and dissenting opinion both used legislative history in support of opposite conclusions in *Babbitt,* and a unanimous Court in *Coke* dismissed the respondent's attempt to use legislative history as simply, "unavailing," without giving much explanation as to why the legislative history was lacking. Putting aside the constitutional question of whether the use of legislative history is a valid method to ascertain Congress' intent, the use of legislative history did not seem especially useful for Breyer, Scalia, or the Court generally, and thus may not help an administrator to understand the meaning of an ambiguous statute as well.

Agency procedures were also not a significant factor for Scalia and Breyer in most cases. Breyer gave attention to the agency procedures in only 4 cases, and Scalia in only 5 cases. A total of only 7 cases gave any attention or weight to the agency procedures. Although the role agency procedures played across all of the cases was limited, the procedures did serve as a safeguard and afforded the agency more discretion in some instances. For example, Breyer explains in the *Coke* unanimous opinion that the DOL notice-and-comment rulemaking signaled the procedures employed to define "domestic service employment" and "companionship services" was not merely an interpretive exercise. Instead, the Court reasoned that the rulemaking procedures having taken place was reason enough for the courts to apply *Chevron* deference and give substantial weight to the agency's definitions. Presumably, had the Court decided the rule was merely interpretive, then *Chevron* deference was not warranted and the Court was free to offer a legal opinion on the ambiguous statutory terms de novo.

Coke also offered another interesting facet of how agency rules work by explaining there is a difference between proposed and final rules, and that agencies were free to change their position from proposed rules, so long as the final rules were in-step or reasonable with the proposed rules. Coupling this grant of discretionary power to deviate a final rule from a proposed rule along with the fact that agencies are not necessarily required to act on or incorporate any comments received from the public anyway, provides significant discretionary powers to agencies. In other words, not only are agencies free to ignore public comments received from a notice-in-comment procedure (albeit, the decision to do so could draw criticism from the media and the public), but the final rule the agency implements does not have to take the shape of the proposed rule as advertised.

The *Christopher* decision is a great companion case for *Coke* as it revisits the DOL's attempt to classify a sect of employees (i.e., pharmaceutical detailees) as exempt or non-exempt under the same authorizing statute the Court previously held was ambiguous and thus required broad administrative discretion regarding its interpretation. Scalia's dissent in *Christopher* was in part reasoned by the difference in agency procedures used in *Coke* from that in *Christopher*. In *Christopher*, the majority opinion (which Scalia joined) argued that because the DOL did not undergo notice-and-comment rulemaking, public comment was wrongly absent and the industry was blind-sided with an enormous change of course. The majority emphasized the consequence (i.e., financial burden on industry) as part of the reason why the agency decision was unacceptable; however, it was clear the lack of notice-and-comment played a significant role for Scalia and the majority. The majority opinion pointed out that for 60 years the pharmaceutical industry had acted on the assumption that pharmaceutical employees were exempt. The majority explained the agency's decision to first announce the position that pharmaceutical detailees are non-exempt byway of an amicus brief filed to the Court was not sufficient, and thus the Court in this case elevated the status of bureaucratic representation, transparency, and fairness over administrative efficiency.

Although Breyer consistently granted deference to the agency's position in both cases, his dissenting opinion in *Christopher* did not address the lack of agency procedures raised by the majority at all. Instead, the dissent was focused on the deference owed to the agency as stemming from the previous *Coke* decision which dealt with the very same ambiguous statute. Breyer also gave no attention to the financial impact the new definition would create for the pharmaceutical industry, but instead offered a literalist accounting of the text and the precedent established in *Coke* as the primary reasons the opinion was wrongly decided by the Court. In this case, Breyer's concern over the administrative procedures was entirely replaced with a literalist reading of the statute and a view that the Court's previous decision requiring broad administrative discretion to effectuate the law was already established and once again in order. In short, Breyer and Scalia seemed to adopt one another's opposite theoretical approach in actual application.

The *Fox Television Inc*., also offered a glimpse into the minds of Scalia and Breyer regarding the importance of agency rulemaking for determining whether agency actions are valid. In this case Breyer and Scalia share a written exchange on the topic of how notice-and-comment procedures fit with the Court's arbitrary and capricious standard. Recall, Breyer's dissent explains courts should reach the same conclusion regarding whether an agency action was arbitrary and capricious regardless if the agency action was the result of notice-and-comment rulemaking or adjudication. For Breyer, the agency's change of position on fleeting expletives required thorough explanation and the route the agency takes (rulemaking or adjudication) should make no difference to the court's decision of whether the action was arbitrary and/or capricious. Scalia disagrees, and explains it is not necessary to incorporate all of the APA's notice-and-comment procedural requirements into review of agency adjudicatory decisions under the arbitrary and capricious standard. Once again, Scalia gives weight to the agency procedures as partly why the agency decision was permissible. Similar to the holding in *Coke*, Scalia argues that an agency change of opinion is permissible so long as its explanation for change is reasonable. Scalia continues by explaining an agency is not required to give a "heightened" review or explanation demonstrating a new opinion is better than a previously held agency opinion, but only need to show it is within reason. In *Perez* Scalia makes a plea of the importance of notice-and-comment rules when he offers a warning that if courts continue the dangerous precedent of deferring to agency interpretations of their own regulations, it is likely that agencies will promulgate interpretive rules to avoid notice-and-comment oversight.

In summary, each Justice's approach to the role of administrative procedures as affording or limiting administrative discretion varied. For example, although Breyer wrote separately in *Coeur Alaska, Inc.* to explain the EPA's administrative discretion was kept in check due to the agency procedures that allowed the EPA to veto the Corp's permitting decisions, Breyer ignored the lack of procedures in *Coke* and instead emphasized stare-decisis and the need for agency expertise and interpretation as a way to embolden agency discretion. Similarly, Scalia's dissent in *Oregon* arguing the lack of notice-and-comment procedures as not limiting the Attorney General's interpretive rule is hard to reconcile with his *Coeur Alaska, Inc.* vote which emphasized notice-and-comment rules as signaling administrative discretion, or the *Sandoval* opinion he authored which emphasized administrative discretion as limited due to the procedural requirements attached to the agency byway of the authorizing legislation.

Pertinent

The next of Rohr's pillars used to dissect the cases is the "pertinent" aspect of Court decisions. As Rohr explains, Court opinions are relevant and deal with real-world problems, thus offering a meaningful way for administrators to attempt to understand how the law intersects with agency actions. For the purposes of this book focusing on administrative actions, pertinence is used herein to highlight the various types of administrative actions found in this review and how each Justice approaches these different actions. Those actions included notice-and-comment rulemaking, interpretive rules, statutory interpretation, and agency inaction. Each of these actions serve as tools available to public administrators, and are thus pertinent and relevant from an administrative point of view. Therefore, Scalia's and Breyer's judicial approach regarding these agency actions are measured below to see how their jurisprudence affects administrative discretion in these varying contexts.

Notice-and Comment Rulemaking

A total of 6 cases (*O'Hagan, Babbitt, Brown, National Association of Homebuilders, Coke,* and *Perez)* dealt with a legal issue that to some extent stemmed from an agency's notice-and-comment procedures. Although there were other cases that included discussions on the role of notice-and-comment procedures, in only these 6 cases did an agency actually employ notice-and-comment procedures, or in the case of *Perez*, the lack of employing notice-and-comment procedures was the focus of the case. Breyer and Scalia voted together for the *Coke* case (albeit in *Coke*, Scalia wrote a separate concurring opinion distinguishing his position on judicial review of administrative actions from that of Breyer) and the unanimous *Perez* case. Breyer sided with the agency's position in 5 of the 6 cases and voted to empower the agency's regulatory reach in all 6 cases. In contrast, Scalia sided with the agency's position in only 3 of the 6 notice-and-comment cases and voted to empower the regulatory aims of the agency in only 2 cases. Interestingly, despite these cases involving notice-and-comment procedures, Scalia emphasized the agency procedures as part of the reasoning for the decision in only 2 cases, and Breyer in only 1 instance.

The most interesting case highlighting notice-and-comment rulemaking was the *National Association of Homebuilders* case as the Court's view of the agency rule was also used to distinguish discretionary acts from non-discretionary acts. Recall, the FSW and NMFS regulation promulgated through notice-and-comment procedures adopted language stating ESA requirements attaching to federal agencies "applies to all actions in which there is discretionary federal involvement or control." The majority opinion (joined by Scalia) took a very narrow interpretation of the term discretion to show that the EPA's decision to grant Arizona NPDES permitting authority was not a discretionary decision at all, but merely the agency performing its clearly defined statutory duties. Although the Court also used the notice-and-comment regulations to show that affected parties had an opportunity to express their concern, the decision to use the results of the agency rule to further demonstrate the statutory language was novel in that it created what is quite possibly a false dichotomy between discretionary and non-discretionary actions.

Recall in chapter 1, by most accounts, applying a strict definition for administrative discretion for the purposes of administrative law and public administration is troubling given the numerous ways administrators can use discretion (Friendly 1982; Dworkin 1977; Fiss and Rendleman 1984; Shapiro 1983). Breyer and the dissenting Justices were quick to point out the majority's limited depiction of administrative discretion as off the mark. Specifically, Justice Stevens explains in the case at hand that the agency's determination as to whether the statutory criteria are met necessarily requires some discretion and the permitting process alone entails "abounding" discretion. Breyer takes the argument further by explaining "grants of discretionary authority always come with some implicit limits attached" (698). Interestingly, Breyer used the term "discretionary" here to describe an agency's responsibilities under a statute, in opposition to the majority description that the permitting decisions are non-discretionary actions. For Breyer, the actions under statute are discretionary, but agencies are required to go even further in their application of law and look across the federal government to see how their authority functions and conforms to other agencies and competing statutes. Once again, Breyer's calling for functional government along with his hesitancy to offer bright line rules is vividly seen in this opinion as he does not go so far as to create a rule of how agency's should coordinate, but does offer a few hypothetical's to show for example how the FDA would be required to confide with the EPA in the event a new drug under review carried the potential to significantly impact endangered species.

Agency Statutory Interpretation

The next agency action found in the cases reviewed focused on an agency's statutory interpretation. Each case reviewed involves an agency's statutory interpretation to some degree as all agency actions are bound to some extent to the agency's authorizing legislation. In theory, an agency's decision to do or not do essentially anything could be counted as an administrator's interpretation of a statute permitting or forbidding their actions. However, there were 7 cases reviewed (*Alaska, Inc., Harris County, Christopher, Fior D'Italia Inc., Sandoval, Utility Air Regulatory Group*, and *Mead*) whereby the agency's interpretation of a statute was the central focus of the case. Once again, Breyer and Scalia were largely at odds as they voted together in only 1 of the 7 cases (*Coeur Alaska, Inc.*). For these cases, Scalia sided with the agency position and empowered the agency's regulatory power in only 2 cases, whereas Breyer sided with the agency position and empowered the agency's regulatory power in 6 of the 7 cases.

Two factors are considered to assess how each Justice reviewed the agency's interpretation of the statute. First, did the Justice put forth a broad or narrow interpretation of the statute with respect to the agency's position, and did the Justice offer a purposeful view of the authorizing legislation? To the first question, Breyer offered a broad interpretation of the statute in question for 5 of the 7 cases, all of which matched the agency's position. Breyer's narrow interpretation in *Mead* was the only case that was not in agreement with the agency's position. Although Breyer only breaks ranks with the agency in *Mead* regarding this topic, it is clear this opinion was not just an aberration, as Breyer reaffirms his position in *Mead* in multiple cases. Namely, Breyer sets the stage for *Mead* in his prior *Harris County* opinion (which the majority cites as support for the *Mead* decision) as well as his opinion in the *National Cable* case supporting *Mead's* precedent, and his vote in *Oregon* which actually invoked *Mead* to deny *Chevron* deference and his separate opinion in *City of Arlington* that reiterated the jurisdictional question the courts must consider and the importance of *Mead*. Breyer applied a purposeful approach to the law in the *Coeur Alaska, Inc.*, *Sandoval* and *Utility Air Regulatory Group decisions*, all of which also gave a broad reading of the statute and aligned with the agency's interpretation of the statute.

In contrast, Scalia applied a broad reading in 3 of the 7 cases, 2 of which aligned with the agency's position. The broad interpretation that did not match the agency and Breyer's more narrow view was the *Christopher* case whereby Scalia voted with the majority to allow wider coverage of the FLSA than that of the agency. None of the 3 narrow interpretations Scalia offered were in-step with the agency's interpretations. To some extent this separation is predictable, as a narrow interpretation would more often than not constrain an agency's power, something an agency is most likely not want to do. Of course this view rests on an assumption that in most instances the trajectory of public agencies is to grow in regulatory power and strength in part because an agency has an interest to preserve power by giving broad interpretations to ambiguous statutes. Using that assumption, it is not surprising that Scalia's literalist approach—as shown above oftentimes narrowing the statutory meaning—would contrast with an agency's likely more expansive view of their role under the law. Interestingly though, the 7 cases focusing on agency interpretation of statutes also captured a large number of the opinions whereby Scalia offered a consequential or purposive reading of the statute, as 4 of the 7 opinions took a purposive/consequentialist approach. Yet, in only 2 instances that Scalia used a purposive reading did that reading also align with the agency's interpretation of the statute. Thus neither Scalia nor Breyer's use of purpose or consequence are uniformly applied such that an administrator could hope to employ the purposive method to create similar interpretations of ambiguous statutes.

Interpretive Rules

A slightly different agency action very much related to statutory interpretation occurs when an agency promulgates an interpretive rule. Obviously, an interpretive rule is very similar to an agency's statutory interpretation as the rule is merely giving further definition and explanation to a statute. However this action is distinguished here as a separate action because agency interpretive rules are treated differently than other rules and can go further than interpreting a statute (which can vary on a case by case basis) and instead records definitions explaining the agency's policy or stance for future administrative actions. One significant difference regarding interpretive rules is found under the APA, which explains that interpretive rules do not require that an agency undergo notice-and-comment rulemaking. Moreover, courts have long held that interpretive regulations are not offered *Chevron* deference.[18] In other words, the judiciary has distinguished interpretive rules as those rules that merely define statutory terms but do not create binding rules, rights, or obligations anew. Of course, applying strict definitions to say an interpretive versus a legislative rule can be difficult as the definitions alone can significantly impact the range and scope of a decision. For example, the *Coke* decision was a case whereby the DOL simply defined "domestic service employment" and "companionship services," but the regulatory impact resulting from these definitions were immense. Similarly, the EPA's rule aimed at defining the statutory term "harm" seems a mere interpretive ruling, but in both cases the Court held the rulings were beyond interpretive (despite Respondents' and lower Courts' contrary position) and invoked *Chevron* deference, in part because of the rulemaking procedures and binding impact of the agency interpretations on external parties. In short, the varied opinions of the Court itself and the lower courts suggest it is not entirely clear how to identify a purely interpretive rule. Nevertheless, in *Talk America Inc*., *Oregon* and *Perez*, the entire Court agreed were cases dealing with agency interpretive rules.

In both *Talk America Inc.,* and *Oregon* Scalia offered a broad reading of the statute and deferred to the agency's position which also called for increased regulatory power. Although Breyer agreed with the unanimous Court in *Talk America Inc*., that the interpretive rule rendered by the agency was reasonable, Breyer differed from Scalia and provided a narrow reading of the authorizing statute in *Oregon* by not deferring to the agency or calling for additional administrative power. In *Talk America Inc*., the Respondent's specifically argued that the FCC was creating a de facto new regulation through the "guise of interpretation" and called for the Court to provide an interpretation of the statute de novo and not offer deference to the agency interpretation. The unanimous opinion authored by Thomas gave significant textual weight to the open-ended regulatory language "…include, but are not limited to" as evidence the FCC's interpretive rule is in fact interpretive. Although the majority held the FCC's remand order is merely interpretive and "…simply explain[s]…" the interconnection obligation under review, the majority opinion found the agency interpretation as, "neither plainly erroneous nor inconsistent with the regulatory text." Scalia voted with the majority but also heeds a warning concerning the concept of *Auer* deference whereby a court gives deference to an agency's interpretation of their own regulation. Breyer's decision to offer a narrow reading of the statute and invalidate the Attorney General's interpretive rule in *Oregon* can partly be explained by the theme emanating from his jurisprudence calling for a functional approach towards competing statutes and agency coordination. Specifically, Breyer gave weight to the notion that HHS and DOJ need to share statutory responsibilities and work together regarding the management of controlled substances. In *Perez*, both Scalia and Breyer took a narrow approach to the APA such that agencies rendering interpretive rules do not have to undergo notice-and-comment procedures. However, Scalia echoes the *Auer* deference warning again and notes his fear that agencies may increasingly attempt to use interpretive rules as a way to avoid notice-and-comment procedures.

Agency Inaction

A third means of administrative discretion reviewed here was agency inaction. Specifically, the case of *Massachusetts*, and *Norton* were cases whereby the agency decided not to regulate and the Court was asked to compel agency action. Scalia and Breyer agreed with the agency's decision not to act in *Norton* as Scalia wrote a unanimous opinion distinguishing "failure to act" and "denials" and explained that courts are only to review agency's failure to act if the actions are in fact required by law. Even in this latter case though, the Court held that the judiciary could only require the agency to act, but could not go further by defining how the agency should act. Scalia and Breyer also agreed that a court cannot use a random agency statement or document that explicitly states or infers agency action in the future as a required agency action. Rather, an agency may need to change course from planning documents as future budgets are unknown and priorities change over time, thus planning statements or documents are not necessarily a binding commitment for future action that a court can compel an agency to act upon. Both Justices give weight to the practical need for agency's to adapt and the Court warns that to decide otherwise risks injecting, "...the judge into day-to-day agency management" .

The more interesting case involving agency inaction was *Massachusetts* as this was a landmark case with enormous regulatory and economic repercussions. In this case, Breyer takes a different approach towards inaction and calls for the EPA to re-visit the decision to not regulate greenhouse gases. The majority opinion which Breyer joins makes the argument that an agency's decision not to act must be rooted in the statute itself and not issues that are beyond the statute. This point could explain Breyer's departure from *Norton* as the agency inaction in that case was still tied to the statute itself, whereas in *Massachusetts* it is clear the agency was primarily factoring issues not germane to the statute, such as the foreign policy initiatives of the President and the legal precedent set in *Brown.* However, it is also very likely that Breyer was once again putting an emphasis on a functional government by calling for agencies to work together and not in isolation. Specifically, in this case the EPA argued that their reason for inaction was partially because DOT was responsible for regulating fuel emissions, and if the EPA decided to regulate greenhouse gases for new cars, this decision would interfere with the statutory and regulatory obligations of DOT. For the majority opinion and Breyer, this was not a good reason for an agency to "shirk" its responsibilities. Rather, Breyer called for the DOT and EPA to coordinate their regulatory requirements, similar to his decisions in *Coeur Alaska, Inc., National Association of Homebuilders, Utility Air Regulatory Group,* and *Oregon.*

Scalia decided in both cases that agency inaction was valid under the law. In both cases Scalia gives significant deference to an agency's decision not to act and seems to emphasize that the judiciary should generally warrant such respect to agency inaction. This is an interesting position to take as the Court's role in checking an agency's discretion is already limited to those cases actually taken to Court. It stands to reason that most instances whereby the judiciary can provide a check on administrative discretion would come by way of an agency action instead of inaction. Warren (2011) also takes this position when he writes, "action simply because it is action, is more easy to control than inaction, since checks are designed mostly to cope with abusive action, not abusive inaction" (315). In other words, under Scalia's limited role for the judiciary regarding agency inaction, one wonders what checks he deems appropriate to correct capricious or abusive agency inactions. This is a formidable question as some scholars, such as Krislov and Rosenbloom have argued that, "it is not the power of public bureaucracies per se, but their unrepresentative power, that constitutes the greatest threat to democratic government" (1981, 21). Although there were only 2 cases reviewed involving agency inaction, Scalia did write opinions in both instances that suggest his theoretical accounting of judicial deference to agencies generally is actually met in practice when the agency action under review is that of no action at all.

Concrete/Institutional

The final pillars discussed together are Rohr's concrete and institutional pillars explaining how Court decisions are final and carry significant practical ramifications (concrete) as well as embody values developed over time that must continually face new constitutional questions (institutional). The most significant cases demonstrating the very real or concrete effects their specific opinions authored affected regulation and agency discretion were found once again in Breyer's dissent in *Brown* and Scalia's dissent in *Massachusetts* as both of these cases carried the potential to significantly alter the regulatory practices for the respective agencies (FDA and EPA) as well as drastically impact the market economy through such newfound regulatory powers. It is no surprise the *Brown* case sent shockwaves through the federal government given the enormous regulatory aim in question. Recall, the EPA actually cited the prior Court decision in *Brown* as reason why no action was taken regarding greenhouse gas regulation because it was thought that sweeping regulatory changes carrying enormous political and financial impacts on the economy should stem from the legislature directly and not by way of an agency interpretation or rule. The EPA concluded that to regulate greenhouse gases carried the potential to affect the economy even more so than the FDA's attempt to regulate tobacco and thus opted not to regulate. Although this argument held ground for the 5-4 split Court in *Brown*, it carried no weight with Breyer in either the *Brown* or the 6-3 split decision in *Massachusetts.*

Breyer's decisions in both cases demanded a pro-active government that takes on difficult and even politically controversial regulatory problems. In *Brown*, Breyer was quick to dismiss the extensive legislative history (an interpretive tool he advocates for in theory) marshaled by the majority opinion to instead focus on the authorizing legislation in isolation. This alone suggests that the role of legislative history is at least a secondary or perhaps even distant consideration for determining the extent to which administrative discretion should be afforded. More importantly though, this dissent gives a warning to administrators that the requirements of the agency's legislative directive or mission overrides any particular interpretive tools when dealing with statutory and regulatory ambiguity. In other words, the over arching mission of the agency should be at the forefront of an administrators mind, and not the smaller details of ambiguous legal language. Breyer's vote with the majority in *Massachusetts* also shows an agency's inaction does not necessarily warrant additional deference from the Courts and that an administrator's decision to not act should be based on reasoning that meets the statute head-on and not extraneous factors that are only questionably related to the authorizing legislation.

Although Breyer defers to the agency position often and votes to empower agency regulatory power even more-so, Breyer's opinions also demand much of agency's use of discretion. For example, Breyer's vote with the majority in *Massachusetts* agreed that the agency's written opinion explaining the rationale for inaction was not suffice despite the EPA having explained very real difficulties facing the decision to regulate. The EPA concerns expressed in their brief included the challenges of coordinating regulatory responsibilities between EPA and DOT, the President's calling for a comprehensive approach as opposed to a piece-meal approach, and the likely negative effects a short-sighted regulatory scheme may engender—given the early scientific understanding of the issue—on the President's negotiating influence in foreign policy. Yet, these reasons were not enough to deter Breyer's demand for regulatory action. Moreover, the majority and Breyer were not persuaded by Scalia's dissent explaining that even if the EPA's decision for inaction were driven by extraneous factors that go beyond the statute (the primary argument raised by the majority as why inaction was unacceptable), the statute does not prohibit the EPA from deferring a decision to regulate to a later point in time. Not so for Breyer, as administrators must readily address the demands of their legislative purpose and explain reasons for regulatory hesitation with an argument focusing on the statute directly. Combining this view with Breyer's calling for agencies to embody a functional and shared regulatory approach across different agencies as shown in the cases described above in *National Association of Homebuilders, Coeur Alaska, Inc., Utility Air Regulatory Group,* and *Oregon* creates enormous responsibilities on administrators. Recall, Breyer's view in these cases required agencies to look beyond their own authorizing statute(s) and take into account other agency responsibilities and statutory obligations and work alongside those agencies as necessary. From an administrative and practical perspective, decisions such as those move the Court and by extension, citizen expectations, that administrative resolution to complicated regulatory/political issues are optimal. This view empowers administrative discretion, but also places an enormous responsibility on administrators by demanding their discretion is pro-active regarding action and inaction and coordinated across multiple agencies and statutes.

A few of Breyer's opinions also helped the Court to change course as well as give rise to future legislation. For example, Congress soon followed the regulatory route painted by Breyer's dissent in *Brown* by passing the Family Smoking Prevention and Tobacco Control Act in 2009 giving the FDA explicit authority to regulate tobacco. Similarly, Breyer's dissent in *Harris County* helped set the stage for the Court's landmark *Mead* opinion that significantly distinguished the applicability of *Chevron* deference. Recall, Souter's majority opinion in *Mead* explained that the Court has to determine if Congress intended for the executive branch to have the authority to resolve certain statutory ambiguities, and that it should not simply be assumed when statutory ambiguity arises. To bolster this point, Souter cites Breyer's dissent in *Harris County* that reads, "where it is in doubt that Congress actually intended to delegate particular interpretive authority to an agency, *Chevron* is "inapplicable" (596-597). It is interesting to see how a quote from a dissenting opinion can later be used to support future opinions, even those future opinions that significantly change Court precedent. The *Mead* case is a good segway to the concrete and institutional effects brought forth in the Scalia opinions reviewed.

Scalia's dissent in *Mead* exhibited one of his more enduring opinions that may continue to have long-lasting theoretical and practical implications in the future. Although Scalia was merely a lone dissent in this case, this dissent has proven to be a pivotal point of academic and legal interest that is routinely cited regarding the role of judicial review and administrative discretion. To reiterate, Scalia's dissent in *Mead* places a theoretical emphasis on bright line rules to ensure administrative flexibility and help agencies and lower courts forecast how to act with accordance to the Court's expectations. Scalia gives a pragmatic argument that when a Court intervenes and interprets a statute in place of the administrator, the interpretation is binding and forever and will thus constrain an agency's ability to adapt regulations in the future to better meet the authorizing statutes purpose as science and technology improves over time. Scalia advances this argument further in *City of Arlington* when he writes for the majority opinion and explains that the courts are not to determine "jurisdictional" questions regarding authorizing statutes, but should simply assume Congress intended the agency to resolve any ambiguities. In this regard, Scalia supports Friedrich's position that administrative discretion is best constrained through scientific and technological means, rather than by political actors. However, based on the cases reviewed here, the concern that Scalia's broad approach to *Chevron* and disregard for *Mead* may be tempered to some extent, at least for those Judges who also apply a literalist method of statutory interpretation, as the findings here suggest the literalist method (as employed by Scalia anyway) overrides this theoretical accounting and actually diminishes administrative discretion.

Scalia may also impact future courts and the practice of public administration in the future based on the warning he gives in the *Talk America Inc.*, concurring opinion, which he later reiterates in *Perez* and *Decker v. Northwest Environmental Defense Center*[19]. In these cases Scalia gives some credence to the representative values of rulemaking and fairness which reads as an invitation for future courts to challenge the merit of *Auer* deference. If this method of deference were overturned in the future it could significantly re-establish the Court's ability to check administrative actions deriving from interpretations of ambiguous agency rules in the future. Recall, in *Talk America Inc.,* Scalia makes a distinction between the likely effects resultant from *Chevron* and *Auer* deference on the Legislative and Executive branch. Here Scalia advocates for *Chevron* deference in principle by drawing a comparison between *Auer* deference (the precedent set that courts should defer to an agency's interpretation of the agency's own ambiguous rules) to show how *Chevron,* unlike *Auer,* enables administrative flexibility without violating the separation of powers doctrine. In other words, for Scalia, the Court's decision to apply *Chevron* and defer to an agency's interpretation of an ambiguous statute (so long as the interpretation is reasonable) encourages the separation of powers as Congress retains the ability to shape the amount of discretion the agency can assume based on the specificity of the law. According to Scalia, if the courts invoke *Chevron* and Congress disagrees with the amount of discretion afforded to the Executive branch, the courts are thus encouraging Congress to create more specific and less ambiguous laws that will in effect take away administrative power. However, under the *Auer* deference standard, a court's decision to defer to an agency's own regulation encourages agencies to promulgate vague rules and then apply an interpretation that the courts will adhere to given the *Auer* precedent already established. In this instance, Scalia is questioning the merit of courts deferring to agency positions of their own regulations as threatening the democratic values of transparency and predictability of rulemaking generally. For Scalia, the *Auer* deference escapes the intent of rulemaking procedures that promote the democratic processes intended by the APA, and this opinion and subsequent warning offered in other opinions has potential to shift the Court in the future.

The likelihood that the Court will in fact revisit *Auer* deference is given some weight given Alito cited Scalia's concurring opinion warning against the implications of *Auer* deference in *Christopher*. Specifically, Alito explains that deferring to an agency's interpretation of its own ambiguous regulations, "…creates a risk that agencies will promulgate vague and open-ended regulations that they can later interpret as they see fit, thereby 'frustrat[ing] the notice and predictability purposes of rulemaking'"(2168). Alito and Thomas also take up the argument endorsing Scalia's position in *Perez.*

Another enduring opinion authored by Scalia was the dissent in *Massachusetts*. In contrast to Breyer and the majority of the Court, Scalia applauds the notion that the EPA took into account extraneous factors beyond the statute such as foreign policy and the timing concerns of employing regulations while the science of global warming is still only beginning to emerge. Scalia sympathizes with the EPA's attempt to explain their inaction using a 2001 report by the National Research Council (NRC) entitled *Climate Change Science: An Analysis of Some Key Questions.* In that report the agency explains, "there is considerable uncertainty in current understanding of how the climate system varies naturally and reacts to emissions of [GHGs] and aerosols" and continues with other descriptions explaining the science is not yet ready to support regulations with statements such as "current estimate[s] of the magnitude of future warming should be regarded as tentative and subject to future adjustments (either upward or downward)." It is clear that Scalia does not go as far as Breyer in demanding the agency somehow go further to show why the decision to regulate was postponed. Scalia does not understand what the Court is requiring the EPA, and by extension any agency, to do to justify a decision to postpone regulatory measures.

It is clear that Scalia views agency inaction much differently than action, and calls for the courts to suspend judgment of agency inaction unless the law specifically requires an agency take action by a specified point in time. Scalia consistently applied this doctrine of judicial deference to agency inaction in both *Norton* and *Massachusetts.* Some cases reviewed shows that Scalia requires agencies give ample warning of changes in position. For example, in *Christopher*, Scalia went as far as overturning stare-decisis regarding the ambiguity of the FLSA established in *Coke*, primarily because the DOL's change of position on the term pharmaceutical detailee was first announced through an amicus brief and did not undergo notice-and-comment rulemaking. Also, in *Brown* the FDA announced the regulatory measure and received more than 50,000 comments from the citizenry prior to their decision to regulate tobacco and in *Fox Television Inc.*, the decision to change direction on fleeting expletives underwent numerous remand orders and heard complaints from the networks prior to confirming their decision. However, there were counter-examples whereby Scalia voted to allow the agency to switch course without having given public warning through formal or informal rules. For example, neither DOJ (*Oregon* case) nor the Customs Service (*Mead* case) announced their change of course, yet Scalia upheld the agency's new position.

Theory Meets Practice

Reviewing the cases collectively shows that both Justices' jurisprudence in practice does not necessarily flow from their theoretical and contradictory accounting of judicial review of administrative actions. Specifically, Breyer's tendency to defer to agency positions while also requiring more regulatory power and responsibility offsets his theoretical warnings that the judicial branch must take a hard look and subjective and dynamic approach to ensure the bureaucracy does not go beyond their statutory limitations. Similarly, Scalia's theoretical calling for bright line rules (such as *Chevron*) to ensure the separation of powers and limit judicial intervention of agency actions as a way to preserve administrative flexibility was overridden by his literalist approach that narrowed the scope of administrative discretion afforded to agencies. Although both justices had an identifiable jurisprudence, their decisions did not neatly align with their theoretical positions on legal reasoning with regards to judicial review of administrative actions.

Regarding the identifiable jurisprudence, Breyer demanded much of the executive branch; requiring administrative agencies take a functional approach towards interpreting statutes as well as demanding high levels of agency cooperation and coordination. In contrast, Scalia's literalist approach constrained administrative discretion with regard to agency actions, but left broad discretionary powers to agency inactions. The research also showed that an agency's use of procedures (e.g., notice-and-comment rulemaking) and the potential statutory purpose or external consequence sometimes enabled Breyer or Scalia's reasoning to vote a particular way, but these tools did not control decisions. Similarly, the use of legislative history was minimal for both Judges and did not significantly impact the cases or support the Justices' decisions. Instead, the Judge's willingness to adopt a broad or narrow interpretation of the statute in question was a much better indicator of how the Judge would decide the case.

In summary, the aforementioned tools such as agency procedures or legislative history will not hurt the agency's position with respect to the Court, but such tools will not necessarily impact the outcome of the case as they had only a minor role for the Court as well as both Scalia's and Breyer's opinions. Similarly, if an agency attempts to take a purposeful approach to a statute or give weight to potential-external consequences, the agency is not assured a vote from Scalia or Breyer, or other like-minded Judges. In effect, this shows that administrators must necessarily impart the same level of judgment as Judges, and do their best to understand, uphold, and implement their respective laws. To do this, administrators would be wise to use any of the above interpretive tools where possible, but must also acknowledge that there is no template or checklist to find the right answer. Rather, as the term "discretion" implies, to apply discretion effectively requires that some level of judgment is in order!

Revisiting Friedrich and Finer

To bring this project full-circle in light of the cases reviewed, the research offers a final reflection on how Breyer's and Scalia's jurisprudence intersects and contributes to the long debated Friedrich and Finer positions of administrative discretion. Moreover, this discussion explains how their theoretical and practical jurisprudence regarding judicial review of administrative actions are out of step. To begin, Scalia's theoretical descriptions of administrative discretion support Friedrich's calling for empowered agencies to primarily answer to the demands of empiricism and scientific and technological expertise as opposed to political actors. For example, Scalia explains in *Mead, Massachusetts, Harris County, Coeur Alaska, Inc., City of Arlington,* and *Talk America Inc.*, that Judge's are correct to defer to an agency's interpretation and approach towards authorizing statutes in most instances to promote administrative flexibility that can adapt as science and technology improves over time. Theoretically, Scalia does not support the idea of the judicial branch substituting its vision of statutory interpretation in place of the agency as judicial interpretations are binding and prevent the agency's ability to advance regulatory measures that meet new and improved scientific knowledge. In other words, Scalia's stated position reinforces Friedrich's position that administrative expertise is more apt to produce decisions that conform to scientific and technological demands than those decisions resultant from political checks on the executive branch.

However, Scalia's literalist approach supersedes his calling for an empowered executive branch as 10 of the 19 cases reviewed did not empower the agency's regulatory powers. Coupling this finding with the fact that government agencies most often prove victorious in legal battles—in part because of the government's privileged legal status (e.g., sovereign immunity)—shows that the literalist method of interpretation does not compliment the Friedrich position. Instead, the literalist method seems to coincide with Terry's (2002) description that originalism (i.e., literalism) constrains administrative action and authority and reduces an administrator's ability to effectively promote the mission of the agency. In addition, the effects of literalism are not limited to diminishing administrative discretion, but conversely demand much from the legislative branch. Congress would need to draft more specific laws to avoid a literalist Judge's intervention, as the literalist position explored here found that literalism leads to narrow interpretations that do not largely confer administrative discretion to statutory ambiguities. In summary, Scalia's theoretical position supports Friedrich, but his jurisprudence viewed collectively compliments Finer, as Scalia's literalist approach often intervenes and checks the executive branch for cases involving administrative law.

In contrast, Breyer's theoretical position on judicial review of administrative discretion calls for the Judiciary to first determine whether Congress intended agency resolution and then apply a hard look review to determine if the agency action was reasonable. This position was reiterated in the *Coke, National Cable*, *City of Arlington*, and *Harris County* cases, all of which clearly echoed Finer's emphasis on the importance of political checks on administrative discretion. Yet, Breyer's votes empowered the regulatory reach of the agency in 16 of the 19 cases reviewed. Breyer's pragmatic approach gave agencies considerable leeway to resolve regulatory problems, even when the political and economic stakes were very high such as the *Brown* and *Massachusetts* decisions. Moreover, Breyer's functional approach often enabled regulatory solutions as opposed to judicial solutions and demonstrated in multiple cases that he was sensitive to the administrative expertise necessary to resolve complex regulatory problems. For example in *National Association of Homebuilders, Brown, Coeur Alaska Inc., Utility Air Regulatory Group, Oregon,* and *Massachusetts,* Breyer's opinions worked out an interpretation for the authorizing statutes such that the agency could address the administrative problem and not be hindered by a narrow or explicitly-direct reading of the statutory language. In summary, Breyer's theoretical position matches that of Finer, but in practice go much further to support Friedrich and his preference for administrative and scientific expertise as the primary mode of solving regulatory problems.

---

[18]However, a unanimous Court applied *Chevron* to the Department of Treasury's interpretive tax regulations in *Mayo Foundation for Medical Education and Research v. United States* 562 US (2011) which could change the extent to which *Chevron* is applied to interpretive rules.

[19]Justice Breyer did not participate in the hearing of the case and was therefore not included in the overall analysis. However, Scalia offers a detailed analysis in this case of why *Auer* deference is dangerous to the separation of powers and a constitutional democracy.

APPENDIX

Cases Not Selected Due to Legal Question(s) Unrelated to Agency Discretion

Supreme Court Case	Legal Question(s)
Sackett v. E.P.A. 566 U.S. (2012)	Do landowners have a right to judicial review to challenge a compliance order promulgated by the Environmental Protection Agency under the Clean Water Act? A unanimous Court answered affirmatively, but did not decide whether EPA's actions were arbitrary and capricious under the Administrative Procedure Act; violated petitioners' due process, or whether the compliance order used a standard that was unconstitutionally vague as sought by petitioners.
Thompson v. North American Stainless, LP 562 U.S. (2011)	In this case an employee alleged they were fired because the employee's spouse (who works at the same business) filed a sexual discrimination complaint with the Equal Employment Opportunity Commission. The legal question focused on whether the spouse who was fired had standing to sue under the anti-retaliation provision of the civil rights statute given the spouse wasn't the person who actually filed the complaint. A unanimous Court affirmed the spouse has standing, but the case was remanded to the lower courts to review the facts of the case.
Your Home Visiting Nurse Services, Inc. v. *Shalala 525 U.S. 449 (1999)*	Can Medicare-reimbursed health care providers appeal a fiscal intermediary's refusal to reopen previous reimbursement decisions and do they have standing in the federal courts for judicial review? The Court unanimously decided the Board does not have jurisdiction and the petitioner had no standing for judicial review in the federal court system.
Director, Office of Workers' compensation Programs, Department of Labor v. Newport News Shipbuilding and Dry Dock Co. 514 U.S. 122 (1995)	Does the Director of the Labor Department's Office of Workers' Compensation Programs have standing to petition the Court of Appeals for review of a Benefits Review Board decision that denied an individual's disability compensation? A unanimous Court determined the Director lacked standing to appeal the benefits denial because she was not "adversely affected or aggrieved" within the meaning of authorizing statute.

Shalala v. Illinois Council on Long Term Care, Inc. 529 U.S. 1 (2000)	Does an association of nursing homes participating in Medicare have standing to sue the Secretary of Health and Human Services under the Medicare Act challenging various Medicare regulations? A divided Court determined the petitioner did not have standing for judicial review in federal courts, but did not address whether the regulations in question were unconstitutionally vague, promulgated in violation of the Administrative Procedure Act, or violated due process protections as sought by petitioners.
Federal Election Commission v. Akins 524 U.S. 11 (1998)	Do voters have standing to challenge the Federal Election Commission's (FEC) decisions in federal court regarding how a political committee was determined? A divided Court agreed that voters do have standing and are allowed judicial review. However, the specific measures FEC used to support their decision (prompting the lawsuit) were not reviewed. Instead, the Court allowed the agency to address the issue under newly proposed rules.
Ingalls Shipbuilding, Inc. v. Director, Office of Workers' Compensation Programs, Department of Labor 519 U.S. (1997)	Does the surviving spouse of a deceased employee who received disability benefits have access to death benefits given third party pre-death settlements that took place without the employer's approval? A unanimous Court held that the worker's spouse did not forfeit the right to collect death benefits under the LHWCA for failure to obtain the worker's employer's approval of settlements entered into by the worker's spouse with third parties before the worker's death, but no agency actions or decisions were at issue.
U.S. v. Williams 533 U.S. (2008)	Is the Protect Act's "pandering" provision regarding illegal child pornography over broad and in violation of the 1st amendment? A divided Court upheld the Act as Constitutional and not in violation of the 1st amendment or due process claims, but no agency actions or decisions were at issue.
Lebron v. National R.R. Passenger Corp. 513 U.S. 374 (1995)	Petitioner alleged that National Railroad Passenger Corporation (Amtrak) violated the First Amendment by rejecting a billboard display because of the political nature of the advertisement. The legal question was centered on whether Amtrak was a corporation or a government entity. A unanimous Court held that Amtrak is a government entity for purposes of the First Amendment. However the case was remanded to the lower court to determine the facts and issue of the particular case.
City of Erie v. Pap's A.M.529 U.S. 277 (2000)	Does a city's public indecency ordinance prohibiting nude dancing violate the First Amendment? A divided Court determined the city's ordinance does not violate the First Amendment, but no agency actions or decisions were at issue.
Riegel v. Medtronic, Inc 522 U.S. (2008)	Does the Food, Drug, and Cosmetic Act preempt state-law damage claims for injuries caused by medical equipment that was approved by the Food and Drug Administration prior to the product's release to the market?

	In an 8-1 decision, the Court agreed that the federal law preempts the state law claims, but no agency actions or decisions were at issue in this case.
Free Enterprise Fund v. Public Co. Accounting Oversight Board 562 U.S. (2010)	Is the Sarbanes-Oxley Act which put in place the Public Company Accounting Oversight Board, in violation of the Appointments Clause or the separation of powers principle? A divided Court determined the Board's "for cause" provision violated the separation of powers principle by not allowing the President to determine what was "good cause" for removal, but the Board was otherwise permissible and did not violate the Appointments Clause. The legal position of the legitimacy of the agency has no bearing on the agency's methods of implementation.
Woodford v. Ngo 548 U.S. (2006)	Does a prisoner satisfy the Prison Litigation Reform Act's requirement that one must exhaust all administrative remedies prior to filing suit in federal court if the grievance is rejected by the agency for procedural or other non-substantive reasons? A divided Court held one must "properly" exhaust all administrative remedies first. This case focuses on the role of the individual and less so the role of the agency.
National Park Hospitality Association v. Department of Interior 538 U.S. 803 (2003)	Was the National Park Service's rule rendering the Disputes Act of 1978 inapplicable to concession contracts permissible? This would have been a case relevant for this project except that the Court did not decide on the issue, but instead the majority opinion held that the case was not "ripe" for review and there was no concrete
Sims v. Apfel 530 U.S. 103 (2000)	Does a Social Security recipient have standing to petition federal courts regarding issues they failed to address during administrative hearings? A divided Court held that one does not have to exhaust all issues administratively to preserve judicial review. This case focuses on an individual's standing and less so the role of the agency.
Norfold Southern Ry. Co. v. Shanklin 529 U.S. 344 (2000)	Does the Federal Railroad Safety Act of 1970 pre-empt state tort claims? A divided Court held that the Act pre-empts state law and thus railroads cannot be sued under state tort law for alleged- inadequate warning devices at rail crossings if the equipment installed was federally funded. No agency actions or decisions were at issue in this case.
Stone v. I.N.S. 514 U.S. 386 (1995)	Does the filing of a reconsideration motion initiate the running of the 90-day filing period for review of final deportation orders specified in the Immigration and Nationality Act? A divided court held that a reconsideration motion does not toll the running of the 90 day filing period. Although the administrative law judge's decision was at issue, no agency actions were reviewed by the Court.

Mutual Pharmaceutical Co., Inc. v. Bartlett No. 12-142 (2013)	Does federal law preempt a state design defect claim against a generic drug manufacturer? A split Court decided that State-law design-defect claims that turn on the adequacy of a drug's warnings are pre-empted by federal law, but no agency action was under review.
Shinseki v. Sanders 556 U.S. 396 (2009)	Should the Circuit Courts presume a prejudicial error when the Veterans Administration fails to give notice as to who is responsible for producing evidence to substantiate medical claims? A divided court reversed the Federal Circuit's "harmless-error" holdings, but no agency actions or interpretations were in question, only the Circuit Court's framework for reviewing these type of cases.
Bennett v. Spear 520 U.S. 154 (1997)	Do private parties have standing to sue and reverse agency decisions stemming from economic harm due to the Endangered Species Act? A unanimous Court agreed that individuals have standing for such instances but the particular agency actions in this case were not reviewed by the Court.
Decker, Oregon State Forester v. Northwest Environmental Defense Center No.11-338 (2013)	Are petitioners exempt from EPA's permitting requirements? The Court deferred to the EPA's own reasonable interpretation that the permit requirement extends only to traditional industrial sites, such as factories. Although this case was relevant, Justice Breyer did not participate in the hearing of the case and was therefore not included. However, Scalia's dissent for this case is mentioned in a related case, *Perez, Secretary of Labor v. Mortgage Bankers Association*, discussed in chapter 3.

Cases Cited

Alexander v. Sandoval 532 U.S. 275 (2001)
Auer v. Robbins 519 U.S. 452 (1997)
Babbitt v. Sweet Home Chapter of Communities for a Great Oregon 515 U.S. 687 (1995)
Bennett v. Spear 520 U.S. 154 (1997)
Bush v. Gore 531 U.S. 98 (2000)
Cheney v. United States Dist. Court 542 U.S. 367 (2004)
Chevron U.S.A., Inc. v. Natural Resources Defense Council, Inc., 467 U.S. 837 (1984)
Christensen v. Harris County 529 U.S. 576 (2000)
Christopher v. SmithKline Beecham Corp. 567 U.S. (2012)
Citizens to Preserve Overton Park v. Volpe 401 U.S. 402 (1971)
City of Arlington, Texas, et al. v. Federal Communications Commission et al. No. 11-1545 (2013)
*City of Erie v. Pap's A.M.*529 U.S. 277 (2000)
Coeur Alaska, Inc.. v. Southeast Alaska Conservation Council 557 U.S. 261 (2009)
Decker, Oregon State Forester et al., v. Northwest Environmental Defense Center No. 11-338 (2013)
Director, OWCP, DOL v. Newport News Shipbuilding and Dry Dock Co. 514 U.S. 122 (1995)
Federal Election Commission v. Akins 524 U.S. 11 (1998)
Free Enterprise Fund v. Public Co. Accounting Oversight Board 562 U.S. (2010)
FCC v. Fox Television Stations Inc., 556 U.S. 502 (2009)
Food and Drug Administration v. Brown & Williamson Tobacco Corp. 529 U.S. 120 (2000)
Gonzales v. Oregon 546 U.S. 243 (2006)
Ingalls Shipbuilding, Inc. v. Director, Office of Workers' Compensation Programs, Department of Labor 519 U.S. (1997)
Lebron v. National R.R. Passenger Corp. 513 U.S. 374 (1995)
Lochner v. New York, 198 U.S. 75 (1905)
Long Island Care at Home LTD., v. Coke 551 U.S. (2007)
Marbury v. Madison, 5 US 137 (1803)
Massachusetts v. EPA 549 U.S. 497 (2007)

Mayo Foundation for Medical Education and Research v. United States 562 US 704 (2011)
Mistretta v. United States. 488 U.S. 361 (1989)
Morrison v. Olson, 487 U.S. 654 (1988)
Motor Vehicle Manufacturers. Association v. State Farm Insurance 463 U.S. 29 (1983)
Mutual Pharmaceutical Co., Inc. v. Bartlett No. 12-142 (2013)
N. A. v. First Interstate Bank of Denver N.A., 511 U. S. 164 (1994)
National Association of Homebuilders v. Defenders of Wildlife 551 U.S. 644 (2007)
National Park Hospitality Association v. Department of Interior 538 U.S. 803 (2003)
New York vs. United States 342 U.S. 882 (1951).
Norfold Southern Ry. Co. v. Shanklin 529 U.S. 344 (2000)
Norton v. Southern Utah Wilderness Alliance 542 U.S. 55 (2004)
Paralyzed Veterans of America v. D.C. Arena L.P 13-1041 (2015)
Perez, Secretary of Labor, et al. v. Mortgage Bankers Association et al. No. 13-1041 (2015)
Ratzlaf v. United States, 510 U. S. 135 (1994)
Riegel v. Medtronic, Inc 522 U.S. (2008)
Sackett v. E.P.A. 566 U.S. (2012)
Shalala v. Illinois Council on Long Term Care, Inc. 529 U.S. 1 (2000)
Shinseki v. Sanders 556 U.S. 396 (2009)
Sims v. Apfel 530 U.S. 103 (2000)
Skidmore v. Swift & Co., 323 U.S. 134 (1944).
Stone v. I.N.S. 514 U.S. 386 (1995)
Talk America Inc., v. Michigan Bell Telephone Co., 564 U.S. (2011)
Thompson v. North American Stainless, LP 562 U.S. (2011)
TVA v. Hill 437 U.S. 153 (1978)
United States v. Mead Corporation, 533 U.S. 218 (2001)
United States v. Williams 533 U.S. (2008)
United States v. O'Hagan 521 U.S. 642 (1997)
United States v. Fior D'Italia, Inc., 536 U.S. 238 (2002)
Utility Air Regulatory Group v. Environmental Protection Agency et al. No. 12-1146 (2014)
Woodford v. Ngo 548 U.S. (2006)
Your Home Visiting Nurse Services, Inc. v. Shalala 525 U.S. 449 (1999)

References

Appleby, Paul. 1949. *Policy and Administration*. University: University of Alabama Press.

Appleby, Paul. 1952. *Morality and Administration in Democratic Government*. Baton Rouge: Louisiana State University Press.

Baugh, Joyce A. 1989. "Justice Antonin Scalia and the Freshman Effect." Presented at the annual meeting of the Midwest Political Science Association, Chicago, IL.

Beermann, Jack M. 2010. End the Failed Chevron Experiment Now: How Chevron Has Failed and Why it Can and Should be Overruled. *Administrative & Regulatory Law News*, 35(4): 3-15.

Breyer, Stephen. 1986. Judicial Review of Questions of Law and Policy. *Administrative Law Review* 38: 363-398.

Breyer, Stephen. 1992. "1991 Justice Lester W. Roth Lecture: On the Uses of Legislative History in Interpreting Statutes". *Southern California Law Review*. 845-874.

Breyer, Stephen. 2005. *Active Liberty: Interpreting Our Democratic Constitution*. RandomHouse.

Breyer, Stephen. 2010. *Making Our Democracy Work: A Judge's View*. Random House.

Bryner, Gary C. 1987. *Bureaucratic Discretion: Law and Policy in Federal Regulatory Agencies*. Elmsford, NY: Pergamon Press.

Biskupic, Joan. 2009. *American Original: The Life and Constitution of Supreme Court Justice Antonin Scalia*. Sarah Crichton Books

Bressman, Lisa S. 2005. How Mead has Muddied Judicial Review of Agency Action. *Vanderbilt Law Review*. 58: 1441.

Brisbin, Richard A. Jr. 1990. The Conservatism of Antonin Scalia. *Political Science Quarterly* 105: 1- 29.

Brisbin, Richard. 1997. *Justice Antonin Scalia and the Conservative Revival*. Baltimore, MD: Johns Hopkins University Press.

Byellin, Jeremy. 2010. "Westlaw Insider: Insiders Blog, Thoughtful Articles About Legal Research and Westlaw". http://westlawinsider.com/today-in-legal-history/today-in-1994-us-senate-confirms-stephen-breyer-to-the-supreme-court/ (Accessed December 3, 2011).

Cann, Steven J. 1995. *Administrative Law*. Sage Publications, Inc. Thousand Oaks, California.

Cooper, Phillip J. 2000. *Public Law and Public Administration* 3rd edition. Itasca, Illinois: F.E. Peacock Publishers.

Cooper, Phillip J. 2007. *Public Law & Public Administration.* 4th edition. Belmont, CA: Thomson Wadsworth.

Dahl, Robert A. 1970. *After the Revolution? Authority In a Good Society.* New Haven: Yale University Press.

Davis, Kenneth C. 1960. *Administrative Law and Government.* West Publishing Company.

Davis, Kenneth C. 1969. *Discretionary Justice: A Preliminary Inquiry.* University of Illinois Press.

Dodd, Lawrence C., Richard L. Schott. 1979. *Congress and the Administrative State.* New York: John Wiley and Sons.

Donald Barry D., Howard R. Whitcomb. 1981. *The Legal Foundations of Public Administration.* St. Paul, MN: West Publishing Co.

Edelman, Peter B. 1991. Justice Scalia's Jurisprudence and the Good Society: Shades of Felix Frankfurter and the Harvard Hit Parade of the 1950s. *Cardozo Law Review*, 12: 1799-1815.

Eskridge, William, Lauren E. Baer. 2008. The Continuum of Deference: Supreme Court Treatment of Agency Statutory Interpretations from Chevron to Hamdan. *Georgetown Law Journal* 96: 1083.

Frederickson, George H. ed. 1993. *Ethics and Public Administration.* Armonk, NY: M.E. Sharpe.

Frederickson, George H. 1997. *The Spirit of Public Administration.* San Francisco CA: Jossey-Bass.

Friendly, Henry J. 1982. Indiscretion About Discretion. *Emory Law Journal.* 31; 747-764.

Finer, Herman. 1941. Administrative Responsibility in Democratic Government. *Public Administration Review.* p 335-350.

Friedrich, J. Carl. 1940. Public Policy and the Nature of Administrative responsibility. *Public Policy.* Cambridge: Harvard University Press, p 3-34.

Goodnow, Frank J. 1900. *Politics and administration; a Study in Government.* New York. London, Macmillan & Company.

Gulick, Luther. 2005. Notes on the Theory of Organization. *Classics of Organizational Theory.* 6th edition, ed. by Jay M. Shafritz, J. Steven Ott, and Yong Suk Jang, 79-87. Belmont, CA: Wadswroth.

Hyneman, Charles. 1950. *Bureaucracy in a Democracy*. New York: Harper and Brothers.

Hart, H.L.A.1961. *The Concept of Law*. Oxford University Press.

Hargis, Hilla J. 2009. Not to be Overlooked: How the United States Supreme Court Shapes the Administrative State. Dissertation. University of TX at Dallas.

Holmes, Oliver W. 1899. The Theory of Legal Interpretation. *Harvard Law Review*. 12. 417-418.

Howe, Mark D. 1953. *Holmes Laski Letters The Correspondence Of Mr. Justice Holmes And Harold J Laski 1916-1935 II*. Cambridge MA. Harvard University Press.

Horowitz, Donald L. 1977. *The Jurocracy: Government Lawyers, Agency Programs, and Judicial Decisions. Lexington.* Ma: Lexington Books.

Horowitz, R. B. 1994. Judicial Review of Regulatory Decisions: The Changing Criteria. *Political Science Quarterly* 109-133.

Horwitz, Morton J.1957. *The Rise of Legal Realism*. American Journal of Legal History 251-267.

Horwitz, Morton J. 1977. *The Transformation of American Law 1780-1860*. Cambridge Ma: University Press.

Joyce, Walter E.1996. the Early Constitutional Jurisprudence of Justice Stephen G. Breyer: Study of the Justice's First Year on the United States Supreme Court. *Seton Hall Constitutional Law Journal.* 7; 149-163.

Kannar, George. 1990. The Constitutional Catechism of Antonin Scalia. *Yale Law Journal* 1999: 1297-1357.

Keiser, Lael R. 1999. State Bureaucratic Discretion and the Administration of Social Welfare Programs: The Case of Social Security Disability. *Journal of Public Administration Research and Theory.* 9(1): 87–106.

Kersch, Ken I. 2004. Time and the Supreme Court: Justices Brandeis, Brennan, and Breyer, and Constitutional Liberalism. *American Political Science Association.*

Kersch, Ken I. 2003. "The Synthetic Progressivism of Stephen Breyer" *Rehnquist Justice: Understanding the Court Dynamic* (Lawrence, KS: University Press of Kansas).

King, Michael Patrick. 1988. *Justice Antonin Scalia: The First Term on the Supreme Court*-1986-1987. Rutgers Law Journal 20: p1-77.

Kennedy, Duncan. 1973. Legal Formality. *Journal of Legal Studies*. 2: (2) 351- 355.

Lawrence, Solum. 2005. Legal theory Lexicon. http://legaltheorylexicon.blogspot.com/2005/05/legal-theory-lexicon-043-formalism-aand.html, (accessed April 28, 2011).

Lee, Yong S., with David H. Rosenbloom. 2005. *A Reasonable Public Servant: Constitutional Foundations of Administrative Conduct in the United States*. Armonk, NY.

Levin, Ronald M. 2002. Mead and the Prospective Exercise of Discretion. *Administrative Law Review*. 54: 771, 774-76.

Lindblom, Charles E. 1959. The Science of 'Muddling Through'. *Public Administration Review*, 19(2): 79-88.

Llewellyn, Karl. 1962. *Realism in Theory*. Practice Transaction Publishers.

Long, Norton. 1952. Bureaucracy and Constitutionalism. *American Political Science Review* 46(3): 808–18.

Lowi, T.J. 1979. *The End of Liberalism: The Second Republic of the United States*. 2nd ed. New York: Norton.

Lipsky, Michael. 1980. *Street-Level Bureaucracy: Dilemmas of the Individual in Public Service*. New York: Russell Sage Foundation.

Lubbers, Jeffrey S. 1995. Justice Stephen Breyer: Purveyor of Common Sense in Many Forums. *Admin Law Journal* American University 8: 775-776.

Merkel, William G. 2009. The District of Columbia V. Heller and Antonin Scalia's Perverse Sense of Originalism. *Lewis &Clark Law Review*. 13(2): 349-381.

Michael, Sherman D. 1991. The Use of Legislative History: A Debate Between Justice Scalia and Judge Breyer. *Administrative Law News* (1)16.

Miles, Foy H. 2010. Article: On Judicial Discretion in Statutory Interpretation. *American Bar Association Administrative Law Review* (62) 291-327.

Moore, Richter H., and Charles B. Fields. 1988. "Justice Antonin Scalia in the Criminal Arena." Presented at annual meeting of the Southern Political Science Association, Atlanta, GA.

Nagareda, Richard. 1987. The Appellate Jurisprudence of Antonin Scalia. *University of Chicago Law Review* 54: 705-39.

Nelson, Caleb. 2005. What is Textualism? *Virginia Law Review*. 91 (2) 347-418.

Newbold, Stephanie. 2010. Toward a Constitutional School for American Public Administration. *Public Administration Review* 70(4): 538-546.

Oyez Project. 2011. Justice Antonin Scalia. http://oyez.org/justices/antonin_scalia (Accessed May 1, 2011).

Oyez Project. 2011. Justice Stephen Breyer. http://oyez.org/justices/stephen_breyer (Accessed Dec 5, 2011).

Pierce, R., Jr., S. A. Shapiro, and P. R. Verkuil (2004). *Administrative Law and Process*, 4th ed. New York: Foundation Press.

Pierce, Richard J. 1995. Justice Breyer: Intentionalist, Pragmatist, and Empiricist. *Administrative Law Journal* American University 8: 747.

Posner, Richard. 2006. Justice Breyer Throws Down the Gauntlet. *Yale Law Journal.* 115, 1699.

Redford, Emmette S. 1969. *Democracy in the Administrative State.* Oxford University Press.

Rosenbloom, David H. 2000. Retrofitting the Administrative State to the Constitution: Congress and the Judiciary's Twentieth- Century Progress. *Public Administration Review*, 60 (1): 39-46.

Rosenbloom, David H. 2002. *Building a Legislative-Centered Public Administration: Congress and the Administrative State.* 1946-1999.Tuscaloosa, Al: University of Alabama Press.

Rosenbloom, David H. 2003. *Administrative Law for Public Managers*. Boulder, CO: Westview Press.

Rohr, John A. 1986. *To Run a Constitution: The Legitimacy of the Administrative State*. University Press of Kansas.

Rohr, John A. 1998. *Public Service, Ethics & Constitutional Practice*. University Press of Kansas.

Rossum, Ralph A. 1999. The Textualist Jurisprudence of Justice Scalia. *Perspectives on Political Science*. 28(1): 5-6.

Rossum, Ralph A. 2005. The Wit and Wisdom of Justice Scalia. A Review of Scalia Dissents:Writings of the Supreme Court's Wittiest, Most Outspoken Justice by Ring, Kevin A., and The Opinions of Justice Antonin Scalia: *The Caustic Conservative*, by Weizer, Paul I. Claremont Review of Books.

Rossum, Ralph A.2006. *Antonin Scalia's Jurisprudence: Text and Tradition.* University Press of Kansas.

Rubin, Thea F., Albert P. Melone. 1988. Justice Antonin Scalia: A First Year Freshman Effect? *Judicature* 72: 98-102.

Scalia, Antonin.1978. Vermont Yankee: The A.P.A., the D.C. Circuit, and the Supreme Court. *Supreme Court Review*: 345-409.

Scalia, Antonin. 1988. Remarks of Justice Antonin Scalia at Washington, D.C. Panel Discussion of Separation of Powers (audiotape of C-SPAN broadcast, 15 November 1988.)

Scalia, Antonin.1989a. Judicial Deference to Administrative Interpretations of Law. *Duke Law Journal*: 5, 511-21.

Scalia, Antonin.1989b. The Rule of Law as a Law of Rules. *University of Chicago Law Review* 56: 1175-1188.

Scalia, Antonin.1997. *A Matter of Interpretation: Federal Courts and the Law.* Princeton, NJ: Princeton University Press.

Schauer, Frederick. 1988. Formalism. *Yale Law Journal.* 97 :509.

Schoenbrod, D. 1993. *Power Without Responsibility: How Congress Abuses the People Through Delegation.* New Haven, CT: Yale University Press.

Schwartz, Bernard. 1955. Gray vs. Powell and the Scope of Review. *Michigan Law Review*, 54 (1) 1-70.

Selden, Sally C. 1997. *The Promise of a Representative Bureaucracy: Diversity and Responsiveness in a Government Agency.* Armonk, NY: M.E. Sharpe.

Selden, Sally C., Jeffrey L. Brudney, and J. Edward Kellough. 1998. Bureaucracy as a Representative Institution: Toward a Reconciliation of Bureaucratic Government and Democratic Theory. *American Journal of Political Science* 42(3): 717–44.

Shafritz, Jay M., Albert Hyde, and Sandra Parkes, ed. 2004. *Classics of Public Administration.* 5th edition. Belmont, CA: Wadswroth.

Shapiro, Martin. 1983. Administrative Discretion: The Next Stage. *Yale Law Journal.* 92; 1487-1500.

Silverstein Mark, William Haltom. 1996. You Can't Always Get What You Want: Reflections on the Ginsburg and Breyer Nominations. *Journal of Law and Politics.* 12: 459-461.

Simon, Herbert A.1946. The Proverbs of Administration. *Public Administration Review*, 6 (1): 53-67.

Smith, Christopher E. 1993. *Justice Antonin Scalia and the Supreme Court's Conservative Moment.* Praeger Publishers.

Spicer, Michael W. 1995. *The Founders, the Constitution, and Public Administration: A Conflict in World Views.* GeorgetownUniversity Press. Washington D.C.

Staab, James A. 2006. *The Political Thought of Justice Antonin Scalia: A Hamiltonian on the Supreme Court.* Bowman and Littlefield Publishers, Inc.

Strauss, David A. 2008. On the Origin of Rules (with Apologies to Darwin): A Comment on Antonin Scalia's The Rule of Law as a Law of Rules. *University of Chicago Law Review.* 75(3): 997-1013.

Strauss, Peter L.1987. Formal and Functional Approaches to Separation-of-Powers Questions: A Foolish Inconsistency. *Cornell Law Review*. 72: 488- 489.

Sunstein, Cass. 1984. In Defense of the Hard Look: Judicial Activism and Administrative Law. *Harvard Journal of Law and Public Policy* 7. 51-59.

Sunstein, Cass R. 2006. Justice Breyer's Democratic Pragmatism. *Yale Law Journal*. 115: 1719.

Supreme Court official website. http://www.supremecourt.gov/about/biographies.aspx. (Accessed 12/5/12)

Taylor, Frederick W. 2004. Scientific Management. In *Classics of Public Administration.* 5th edition, edited by Jay M. Shafritz, Albert Hyde, and Sandra Parkes, 43-45. Belmont, CA: Wadswroth.

Terry, Larry D. 2003. *Leadership of Public Bureaucracies: The Administrator as Conservator*. 2nd Edition. M.E. Sharpe, Inc., Armonk, New York.

Tushnet. 1985. Anti-Formalism in Recent Constitutional Theory. *Michigan Law Review*. 83. 1502-07.

Unger, R. 1983. The Critical Legal Studies Movement. *Harvard Law Review*. 96: 561-75.

Vermeule, Adrian. 2003. Mead in the Trenches. *George Washington Law Review*. 71:347.

Waldo, Dwight. 1948. *The Administrative State*. New York: Ronald Press.

White, Edward G. 1978. The Evolution of Reasoned Elaboration: Jurisprudential Criticism and Social Change. *Patterns of American Legal Thought*, Indianapolis, IN: Bobbs-Merrill Co.

White, Leonard. 2004. Introduction to the Study of Public Administration. In *Classics of Public Administration.* 5th edition, edited by Jay M. Shafritz, Albert Hyde, and Sandra Parkes,56-63. Belmont, CA: Wadswroth.

Whittington, Keith E. 1999. Constitutional Interpretation: Textual Meaning, Original Intent, & Judicial Review. University Press of Kansas.

Wilson, Woodrow. 1887. The Study of Administration. *Political Science Quarterly*, 2(2):197-222.

Wood, B. Dan, and Richard W. Waterman. 1991. The Dynamics of Political Control of the Bureaucracy. *American Political Science Review* 85 (3): 801–28.

Wyszynski, James Edward Jr. 1989. In Praise of Judicial Restraint: The Jurisprudence of Justice Antonin Scalia. *Detroit College of Law Review*. 117-61.

Index

www.ingramcontent.com/pod-product-compliance
Lightning Source LLC
LaVergne TN
LVHW101441200926
848483LV00001B/13